**Anton Chekhov**

# The Seagull

In a new version by Simon Stephens

A Lyric Hammersmith Production

D1374885

Bloomsbury Methuen Drama
An imprint of Bloomsbury Publishing Plc

B L O O M S B U R Y
LONDON • OXFORD • NEW YORK • NEW DELHI • SYDNEY

**Bloomsbury Methuen Drama**

An imprint of Bloomsbury Publishing Plc

Imprint previously known as Methuen Drama

| | |
|---|---|
| 50 Bedford Square | 1385 Broadway |
| London | New York |
| WC1B 3DP | NY 10018 |
| UK | USA |

**www.bloomsbury.com**

**BLOOMSBURY, METHUEN DRAMA and the Diana logo
are trademarks of Bloomsbury Publishing Plc**

First published 2017

© A new version of The Seagull, 2017

**British Library Cataloguing-in-Publication Data**
A catalogue record for this book is available from the British Library.

ISBN: PB: 978-1-3500-6439-3
ePDF: 978-1-3500-6440-9
eBook: 978-1-3500-6441-6

**Library of Congress Cataloging-in-Publication Data**
A catalog record for this book is available from the Library of Congress.

Series: Modern Plays

Front cover design by AKA

Typeset by Mark Heslington Ltd, Scarborough, North Yorkshire
Printed and bound in Great Britain

To find out more about our authors and books visit www.bloomsbury.com. Here
you will find extracts, author interviews, details of forthcoming events and the
option to sign up for our newsletters.

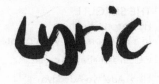

A Lyric Hammersmith production

# THE SEAGULL
# By Anton Chekhov

In a new version by Simon Stephens

First performance of this production at the Lyric Hammersmith
on 03 October 2017

# THE SEAGULL

By Anton Chekhov

In a new version by Simon Stephens

Cast in alphabetical order

Nina **Adelayo Adedayo**
Pauline **Michele Austin**
Jacob **Lloyd Cooney**
Boris **Nicholas Gleaves**
Hugo **Paul Higgins**
Leo **Lloyd Hutchinson**
Irina **Lesley Sharp**
Marcia **Cherrelle Skeete**
Simeon **Raphael Sowole**
Peter **Nicolas Tennant**
Konstantin **Brian Vernel**

Creative Team

Directed by **Sean Holmes**
Design by **Hyemi Shin**
Lighting by **Anna Watson**
Sound by **Pete Malkin**
Casting by **Stuart Burt CDG**
Literal translation by **Helen Rappaport**
Associate Director **Jude Christian**
Assistant Director **Anna Crace**
Movement Consultant **Imogen Knight**

Company Stage Manager **Claire Bryan**
Deputy Stage Manager **Helen King**
Assistant Stage Manager **Lucy Holland**

Senior Producer **Imogen Kinchin**
Producer **Peter Holland**
Assistant Producer **Sarah Georgeson**
Head of Production **Seamus Benson**
Set Construction **Visualscene Ltd.**
Printed Cloth supplied by **Prompt Side**
Costume Supervisor **Katie Salmon**
Irina's jewellery supplied by **Ros Badgers** (www.badgersvelvet.com)
Pauline's wig by **Susanna Peretz**

Press Agency **Jo Allan PR**
Marketing Design **AKA**

**With thanks to**
Fisayo Akinade, Adjoa Andoh, Leo Bill, Sacha Dhawan, Joan Iyiola, John
Lightbody, Daniel Mays, Sophie Melville, Tanya Moodie, David Moorst, Sarah
Niles, Katherine Pearce, Billy Seymour, Nathaniel Wade, Danny Webb and
the Royal Court.

## ANTON CHEKHOV

Russian writer Anton Chekhov is recognized as a master of the modern short story and a leading playwright of the late 19th and early 20th centuries.

Anton Chekhov was born on 29 January 1860, in Taganrog, Russia. Through stories such as 'The Steppe' and 'The Lady with the Dog,' and plays such as *The Seagull* and *Uncle Vanya*, the prolific writer emphasized the depths of human nature, the hidden significance of everyday events and the fine line between comedy and tragedy. Chekhov died of tuberculosis on 15 July 1904, in Badenweiler, Germany.

## SIMON STEPHENS

Simon is an award-winning playwright.

FOR THE LYRIC: *Fatherland* (Manchester International Festival 2017/Lyric Hammersmith & LIFT Festival 2018), *Herons, Morning* (also Traverse, Edinburgh), *Three Kingdoms* (also Tallinn/Munich), *A Thousand Stars that Explode in the Sky* and *Punk Rock* – winner 2009 *Manchester Evening News* Award for Best Production (also Manchester Royal Exchange and UK tour).

OTHER THEATRE CREDITS INCLUDE: *The Threepenny Opera* (National Theatre); *Heisenberg* (Manhattan Theatre Company/Wyndham's, Elliott & Harper Productions); *Obsession* (Barbican/Toneelgroep Amsterdam); *Song From Far Away, The Cherry Orchard, I Am The Wind* (Young Vic); *Carmen Disruption* (Deutsches Schauspielhaus/Almeida); *Nuclear War, Birdland, Wastwater* – winner 2011 Theater Heute's Award, *Motortown* – winner 2007 Theater Heute's Award, *Country Music, Herons, Bluebird* (Royal Court); *The Curious Incident Of The Dog In The Night-Time* – Winner Olivier and Tony Awards for Best New Play (National Theatre /Apollo /Gielgud /Barrymore Theatre, Broadway); *A Doll's House* (Young Vic/Duke Of York's); *Pornography* – winner 2008 Theater Heute's Award (Deutsches Schauspielhaus/Edinburgh Festival/Birmingham Rep/Tricycle Theatre); *Sea Wall* (Bush/National Theatre); *Harper Regan, Port* – winner 2001 Pearson Award for Best Play (Royal Exchange/National Theatre) and *On The Shore Of The Wide World* – winner 2005 Olivier Award for Best New Play (Royal Exchange).

FILM AND TELEVISION CREDITS INCLUDE: *Dive, Pornography* and *Cargese*.

RADIO CREDITS INCLUDE: *Five Letters Home to Elizabeth* and *Digging*.

Simon is an Artistic Associate at the Lyric Hammersmith and Associate Playwright at the Royal Court. He was also on the board for Paines Plough between 2009 and 2014, and was a Writers' Tutor for the Young Writers' Programme at the Royal Court between 2001 and 2005.

## THE COMPANY

### CAST in alphabetical order

### ADELAYO ADEDAYO (Nina)

THEATRE CREDITS INCLUDE: *Cuttin' It* (Young Vic/Royal Court); *Klippies* (Southwark Playhouse); *Rachel* (Finborough Theatre) and *The Dead Wait* (Park Theatre).

FILM AND TELEVISION CREDITS INCLUDE: *Unlocked, Timewasters, Houdini & Doyle, Some Girls, Stan Lee's Lucky Man, Law & Order UK, Skins, Gone Too Far, Sket, MI High, Meet The Bandaiis* and *The Bill.*

### MICHELE AUSTIN (Pauline)

THEATRE CREDITS INCLUDE: *Medea* and *The Chain Play* (Almeida); *Pride and Prejudice* (Sheffield Crucible Theatre); *The House That Will Not Stand* and *The Riots* (Tricycle); *I Know How I Feel About Eve* (Hampstead Theatre); *To Kill A Mockingbird* (Regent's Park Open Air Theatre); *Sixty-Six Books* (Bush); *Wild Child* (Rough Cuts); *The Lost Mariner, Been So Long* and *Breath, Boom* (Royal Court); *Generations* (Young Vic); *Out In The Open* (Hampstead); *Our Country's Good* (Out of Joint) and *It's A Great Shame* (Stratford East).

FILM AND TELEVISION CREDITS INCLUDE: *The Children Act, What We Did On Our Holidays, Another Year, The Infidel, All Or Nothing, I'll Sleep When I'm Dead, Second Nature, Secrets & Lies, EastEnders, The Coroner, The Casual Vacancy, Death In Paradise, Harry And Paul, Holby City, Peep Show, Silent Witness, Britannia High, Outnumbered, Never Better, Secret Life, The Bill, The Wife Of Bath, Clare In The Community, Doctors, Gimme Gimme Gimme, Babes In The Wood, Kiss Me Kate* and *The Perfect Blue.*

### LLOYD COONEY (Jacob)

THEATRE CREDITS INCLUDE: *A Christmas Carol* (The Ark); *The Plough and the Stars, The Shadow of a Gunman, Twelfth Night* and *The Risen People* (Abbey Theatre, Dublin); *The Windstealers* (Smock Alley); *The Waste Ground Party* (Peacock Theatre); *Angel Meadow* (HOME); *Thirteen, Living The Lockout* and *The Boys of Foley Street* (A.N.U. Productions); *Romeo and Juliet* (The Complex, Dublin); *Delta Phase* (Theatre Upstairs) and *Reality Shows* (Project Arts Centre).

FILM AND TELEVISION CREDITS INCLUDE: *Charlie, The Execution* and *The Shadowboxer.*

## NICHOLAS GLEAVES (Boris)

FOR THE LYRIC: *Chair and The Under Room.*

OTHER THEATRE CREDITS INCLUDE: *The Father* (Wyndham's); *Light Shining in Buckinghamshire* (National Theatre); *Macbeth* (Manchester Royal Exchange); *On The Shore of the Wide World* (Manchester Royal Exchange/ National Theatre); *As You Like It, Macbeth* and *Othello* (Ludlow Festival); *The Front Page* (Donmar), *Dear Elena Sergeevna* (Gate); *Dark Glory* (Nuffield Southampton) and *Sixty-Six Books* (Bush).

FILM AND TELEVISION CREDITS INCLUDE: *Nightstand, United Passions, A Congregation of Ghosts, Fallout, Chatroom, Incendiary, Cold Feet, Marvellous, Scott & Bailey, Ashes to Ashes, Survivors, City Lights, Playing the Field, Public Enemies, Reunited, Murderland* and *Foyle's War.*

## PAUL HIGGINS (Hugo)

THEATRE CREDITS INCLUDE: *Temple, Luise Miller, The Cosmonaut's Last Message* (Donmar); *Blackbird, King Lear* (Citizens); *Hope, Nightsongs, American Bagpipes, The Conquest of the South Pole* (Royal Court); *Children of the Sun, White Guard, Paul, An Enemy of the People, The Hare Trilogy* (National Theatre); *Damascus* (Traverse/Tricycle/Middle East); *The Tempest* (Tron); *Black Watch* (National Theatre of Scotland); *Macbeth, Conversations After A Burial* (Almeida); *Measure for Measure* (RSC); *The Golden Ass, A Midsummer Night's Dream* (Shakespeare's Globe).

FILM AND TELEVISION CREDITS INCLUDE: *Victoria & Abdul, Line of Duty, Decline and Fall, The Thick of it, New Town, The Last Enemy, Murder, Raised By Wolves, Utopia, Low Winter Sun, Couple in a Hole, In The Loop, Red Road, Bedrooms and Hallways, Apostle* and *The Party's Just Beginning.*

## LLOYD HUTCHINSON (Leo)

FOR THE LYRIC: *The Birthday Party, Three Sisters.*

OTHER THEATRE CREDITS INCLUDE: *Salome, The Plough and the Stars, Husbands & Sons, The Beaux Stratagem, Collaborators, The Observer* and *Once In A Lifetime* (National Theatre); *A Midsummer Night's Dream* and *A Respectable Wedding* (Young Vic); *Little Revolution, Measure for Measure* and *The Lightning Play* (Almeida); *A View From The Bridge* (Liverpool Playhouse); *The Orphan of Zhao, Boris Godunov* and *Travesties* (RSC); *A Particle of Dread* (Off Broadway); *A Flea In Her Ear* (The Old Vic); *Life Is A Dream* (Donmar); *The Taming Of The Shrew* (Manchester Royal Exchange); *Rhinoceros* and *One for the Road* (Ambassadors).

FILM AND TELEVISION CREDITS INCLUDE: *The Little Stranger, Catastrophe, White Gold, Silent Witness, Utopia, Casualty, Hatfields & McCoys, Hustle, Titanic, The Fades, Silk, Florence Foster Jenkins, Anonymous* and *Mrs Henderson Presents.*

**LESLEY SHARP** (Irina)

THEATRE CREDITS INCLUDE: *A Taste of Honey, Harper Regan, Mother Courage and her Children, Murmuring Judges, Uncle Vanya* – Olivier Award nomination for Best Supporting Actress (National Theatre); *Top Girls, The Recruiting Officer, Road* and *Our Country's Good* (Royal Court); *Ghosts* (Duchess); *Little Voice* (Vaudeville); *God Of Hell, A Family Affair* – Olivier Award nomination for Best Comedy Performance (Donmar); *Playing With Trains* and *Mary and Lizzie* (RSC) and *Summerfolk* (Chichester Festival Theatre).

FILM AND TELEVISION CREDITS INCLUDE: *Three Girls, Scott & Bailey, Capital, Starlings, The Shadow Line, Whistle and I'll Come To You, Cranford, The Diary of Anne Frank, Doctor Who, Afterlife, Planespotting, Carla, Carrie's War, Bob and Rose, Clocking Off, Great Expectations, Playing The Field, Common as Muck, Inkheart, Vera Drake, Cheeky, From Hell, The Full Monty, Naked, Priest, Close My Eyes, The Rachel Papers, Rita, Sue and Bob Too* and *The Love Child.* Lesley also stars in the new Sky1 comedy *Living the Dream.*

**CHERRELLE SKEETE** (Marcia)

THEATRE CREDITS INCLUDE: *Harry Potter and the Cursed Child* (Palace); *Three Days in the Country* and *Amen Corner* (National Theatre); *Wind in the Willows* (Royal and Derngate, Northampton); *And I and Silence* (Finborough) and *The Lion King* (Lyceum).

FILM AND TELEVISION CREDITS INCLUDE: *Doctors, Silent Witness, Danny and the Human Zoo, The Five, Ordinary Lies* and *Call the Midwife.*

**RAPHAEL SOWOLE** (Simeon)

THEATRE CREDITS INCLUDE: *Pygmalion* (Headlong UK Tour); *Hamlet* (Black Theatre Live UK Tour); *Measure for Measure* (Young Vic) *The Merchant of Venice* (Almeida); *Tis Pity She's A Whore* (Cheek by Jowl/Barbican) and *A Clockwork Orange* (Theatre Royal Stratford East).

FILM AND TELEVISION CREDITS INCLUDE: *Black Mirror, Starred Up, Trainees, Edge of Heaven* and *Youngers.*

**NICOLAS TENNANT** (Peter)

FOR THE LYRIC: *Three Kingdoms* (also Tallinn/Munich).

THEATRE CREDITS INCLUDE: *Curious Incident Of The Dog In The Night-Time* (Gielgud); *Hamlet, Taming Of The Shrew, King Lear, As You Like It* and *All's Well That Ends Well* (RSC); *The Alchemist* and *Dr Faustus* (Liverpool Playhouse); *Tiger Country* and *Love Me Tonight* (Hampstead); *The Ragged Trousered Philanthropists* (Liverpool Everyman /Chichester); *The Power Of Yes, The Blue Ball* and *The U.N. Inspector* (National Theatre); *Roaring Trade* and *Piranha Heights* (Soho); *People At Sea* (Salisbury Playhouse); *Caucasian*

*Chalk Circle* (National Theatre/Tour); *Under The Black Flag* (Shakespeare's Globe); *Members Only* (Trafalgar Studios) ; *Dead Funny* (West Yorkshire Playhouse); *Cloud 9* and *Teeth 'N' Smiles* (Sheffield Theatre) and *Bad Company, Sugar, Sugar* and *Love & Understanding* (Bush).

FILM AND TELEVISION CREDITS INCLUDE: *Peaky Blinders, The Bill, The Gift, The Fool, Nice Town, Between the Lines, Breaking the Bank, Oscar & Lucinda, Friday On My Mind, Backbeat* and *Terry Pratchett's The Colour of Magic.*

## BRIAN VERNEL (Konstantin)

THEATRE CREDITS INCLUDE: *Barbarians* (Young Vic); *Future Conditional* (The Old Vic); *Takin' Over the Asylum* (Royal Lyceum/Citizen's); *The Static, Blackout* (ThickSkin) and *Four Parts Broken* (National Theatre Of Scotland/ Traverse /Oran Mor).

FILM AND TELEVISION CREDITS INCLUDE: *Dunkirk, Papillon, Star Wars: The Force Awakens, Winter Song, Offender, Let Us Prey, Collateral, The Tunnel, Doctor Who, The Missing 2, The Last Kingdom, The Casual Vacancy, Grantchester, Prey* and *The Field of Blood.*

## CREATIVE TEAM

### SEAN HOLMES (Director)
Sean is Artistic Director of the Lyric Hammersmith.

FOR THE LYRIC: *Terror, Shopping and Fucking, Bugsy Malone, A Midsummer Night's Dream* (UK Tour/Manchester Royal Exchange/Brisbane Festival/Dublin International Festival), *Herons, Secret Theatre Shows 1, 2, 3, 5* and *7, Cinderella, Desire Under the Elms, Morning, Have I None, Saved, Blasted* – winner Olivier Award 2011, Outstanding Achievement in an Affiliate Theatre, *A Thousand Stars Explode in the Sky, Ghost Stories* (also Duke of York's/Liverpool Playhouse/Panasonic Theatre, Toronto/Arts Theatre), *Three Sisters* and *Comedians*. In 2016 Sean directed *The Plough and the Stars* at the Abbey Theatre, Dublin (also Irish/US Tour). Sean was an Associate Director of the Oxford Stage Company from 2001 to 2006 and has also worked at the National Theatre, RSC, Tricycle, Royal Court, Donmar Warehouse, Chichester Festival Theatre and the Abbey Theatre, Dublin.

### HYEMI SHIN (Designer)
FOR THE LYRIC: *Secret Theatre shows 1, 2, 4, 5, 6, 7, Herons, A Midsummer Night's Dream* (also UK Tour/Manchester Royal Exchange/Brisbane Festival/Dublin International Festival – Linbury Prize winner 2011), *Morning* (also Traverse, Edinburgh), *Desire under the Elms* (costumes).

OTHER THEATRE CREDITS INCLUDE: *Once in a Lifetime, Sizwe Banzi is Dead* and *Dirty Butterfly* (Young Vic); *Swan Lake – Loch na hEala* (costumes for Michael Keegan Dolan Dance Company, Dublin Festival and Sadler's Wells – winner Best Costume Design, *Irish Times* Theatre Awards); *Made Visible* (The Yard); *The Brink* (Orange Tree); *Playland* and *He Wore A Red Hat* (New Perspectives Theatre); *Life's Witness* (Linbury Studio ROH2); *Unearth* (National Ballet of Canada); *The Kreutzer Sonata* (Ballet Moscow).

### ANNA WATSON (Lighting Design)
FOR THE LYRIC: *Shopping and Fucking.*

THEATRE CREDITS INCLUDE: *King Lear* (Shakespeare's Globe); *Becoming: Part One, Salt, Root and Roe* (Donmar); *The Roaring Girl, Snow in Midsummer* (RSC); *Dutchman, The Secret Agent, Fireface, Disco Pigs, Sus* (Young Vic); *You for Me for You, Plaques & Tangles, A Time to Reap* (Royal Court); *The Chronicles of Kalki* (The Gate); *Bank on it* (Theatre-Rites / Barbican); *On the Record, It felt empty when the heart went at first, but it's alright now* (Arcola); *Paradise, Salt* (Ruhr Triennale, Germany); *Gambling, This Wide Night* (Soho Theatre); *Rutherford and Son, Ruby Moon* (Northern Stage); . . . *Sisters* (Headlong); *King Pelican, Speed Death of the Radiant Child* (Drum, Plymouth).

OTHER CREDITS INCLUDE: *Don Carlo* (Grange Park); *Orlando* (WNO and Scottish Opera); *Ruddigore* (Barbican, Opera North and UK Tour); *Critical Mass* (Almeida); *Songs from a Hotel Bedroom, Tongue Tied* (Linbury Studio ROH2); *The Bartered Bride* (Royal College of Music); *Against Oblivion* (Toynbee Hall).

DANCE CREDITS INCLUDE: *Mothers* (The Place); *Refugees of a Septic Heart* (The Garage); *Soul Play* (The Place); *View from the Shore / Animule Dance* (Clore ROH).

## PETE MALKIN (Sound Design)
FOR THE LYRIC: *Space Junk* (with Gameshow).

THEATRE CREDITS INCLUDE: *Frogman* (Curious Directive); *Twelfth Night* (Manchester Royal Exchange); *The Kid Stays In The Picture* and *The Encounter* (Complicité); *Home Chat* (Finborough); *The Tempest* (Donmar); *Andrea Chenier* (Opera North); *Ungeduld des Herzens* (Schaubühne and Complicité); *Unearthed* (Arcola Theatre and UK Tour); *7 – 75* (The Place); *Am I Dead Yet* (Unlimited Theatre and Bush); *War Correspondents* (Greenwich Festival and UK Tour); *The Commission* (ROH, Aldeburgh and Opera North); *SUN* (St Leonard's Church/National Art Service); *Farragut North* (Southwark Playhouse); and *The Noise* (Northern Stage and Unlimited).

ASSOCIATE SOUND DESIGNER CREDITS INCLUDE: *Harry Potter and the Cursed Child* (Palace); *1984* (Headlong); *Oresteia* (Trafalgar Studios); *Hamlet* (RSC).

FILM AND TELEVISION CREDITS INCLUDE: *The Rochdale Pioneers.*

## STUART BURT CDG (Casting)
FOR THE LYRIC: *Terror* (also Brisbane Festival).

THEATRE CREDITS INCLUDE: *Uncle Vanya* (Theatr Clwyd/Sheffield Crucible); *Buried Child, The Spoils* (Trafalgar Studios); *The End of Longing, Women on the Verge of a Nervous Breakdown* (Playhouse); and *Passion Play* (Duke of York's); *Blue/Orange, Private Lives, Gaslight, Dirty Rotten Scoundrels, The Rocky Horror Show, Annie Get Your Gun, Tonight's The Night, Spamalot* (UK Tour); and *The Choir* (Glasgow Citizens/UK Tour).

AS CASTING DIRECTOR FOR THE JAMIE LLOYD COMPANY CREDITS INCLUDE: *Doctor Faustus* (Duke of York's); *The Maids, The Homecoming, The Ruling Class, Richard III, Macbeth* (Trafalgar Studios); *East is East, The Pride* (Trafalgar Studios/UK Tour).

Stuart is a member of the Casting Director's Guild of Great Britain and Ireland.

**JUDE CHRISTIAN** (Associate Director)
FOR THE LYRIC: *Seventeen, Shopping and Fucking, Aladdin.*

AS DIRECTOR, THEATRE INCLUDES: *Parliament Square* (Manchester Royal Exchange); *Bodies, Lela & Co.* (Royal Court); *The Darkest Corners* (Transform); *The Path* (Hightide); *Blue* (RWCMD); *Split/Mixed* (Summerhall); *How Do You Eat An Elephant/Bwyta Eliffant, Sut Mae Gwneud Hynny Dwedwch?* (National Youth Theatre of Wales); *Happy, The Mushroom* (Pentabus Young Writers' Festival); *Punk Rock, Last Easter* (RADA); *I'd Rather Goya Robbed Me of My Sleep than Some Other Arsehole* (Gate, Boom Arts); *Balansera* (Poole Lighthouse); *Sonata Movements* (Blue Elephant).

OPERA CREDITS INCLUDE: *©alculated to Death* (Tête-à-Tête Festival), *Hidden in Plain Sight* (Académie du Festival d'Aix-en-Provence).

AS ASSOCIATE DIRECTOR, THEATRE INCLUDES: *Carmen Disruption* (Almeida).

Jude is an Artistic Associate at the Gate Theatre, The Yard Theatre and the Lyric Hammersmith.


**IMOGEN KNIGHT** (Movement Consultant)
FOR THE LYRIC: *Seventeen.*

THEATRE/OPERA CREDITS INCLUDE: *The Winter's Tale, Powder Her Face* (ENO); *Amadeus, The Threepenny Opera, Les Blancs, I Want My Hat Back, Edward II, Dido, Queen Of Carthage* (National Theatre); *The Emperor, Measure For Measure, Dirty Butterfly* (Young Vic); *Our Ladies Of Perpetual Succour* (National Theatre of Scotland/ National Theatre/UK tour/West End); *Red Velvet* (Garrick); *Nuclear War* (as Director), *Linda, God Bless The Child, The Low Road, A Time To Reap* (Royal Court); *Who's Afraid Of Virginia Woolf* (West End); *The Skriker* (Manchester International Festival/Royal Exchange); *Against, Carmen Disruption, Little Revolution, Turn Of The Screw, King Lear, Measure For Measure, When The Rain Stops Falling* (Almeida); *Knives in Hens* (Donmar); *Hamlet, Blindsided, Cannibals* (Royal Exchange); *In Time O'strife, An Appointment With The Wicker Man, The Missing* (National Theatre of Scotland); *The Crucible* (The Old Vic); *Pests* (Clean Break, Royal Exchange, Royal Court/UK Tour); *The Little Sweep* (Malmo Opera).

FILM AND TELEVISION CREDITS INCLUDE: *The Innocents* (Netflix), *On Chesil Beach* (Golam Films); *Harlots* (ITV); *Call The Midwife, The Hollow Crown* (BBC).

Bugsy Malone

Herons

A Midsummer Night's Dream

Terror

The Lyric Hammersmith is one of the UK's leading producing theatres. For more than one hundred and twenty years it has been responsible for creating some of the UK's most adventurous and acclaimed theatrical work. It has gained a national reputation for its work with and for children and young people and creates pathways into the arts for young talent from all backgrounds, helping to diversify our industry. Recent productions include our critically acclaimed annual pantomimes, the smash hit *Bugsy Malone*, the international tour and co-production with Filter Theatre of *A Midsummer Night's Dream* and the UK premiere of the international phenomenon, *Terror*.

The Lyric's dual commitment to producing the highest-quality contemporary theatre, whilst nurturing the creativity of young people, is what makes it unique within the cultural ecology of the UK. It is a local theatre rooted in its community with a national and international reputation for the quality and innovation of its artistic work.

In April 2015 the Lyric reopened following a multi-million pound capital project, which saw the addition of the Reuben Foundation Wing housing state-of-the-art facilities for theatre, dance, film, music, digital and more. The 'new' Lyric is now the largest creative hub in West London and home to an innovative partnership of like-minded leading arts organisations that work together to deliver life-changing creative opportunities for thousands of young West Londoners.

Supported by

h&f
hammersmith & fulham

Supported by
ARTS COUNCIL
ENGLAND

Registered Charity, No. 278518

# LYRIC HAMMERSMITH SUPPORTERS

Thank you to all our wonderful supporters who donate to the Lyric's work on and offstage. We couldn't do it without you.

## LOVE THE LYRIC
Anonymous
Sian & Rob Alexander
Carrie & John Armstrong
Laura & John Banes
Lucy Bennell
Guillaume & Carole Bonpun
Lisa Burger
The Callanan Family
Deborah Durkin
Mike Dibb & Cheli Duran
Andrew & Lindsay Elder
Caroline Elliot
Liz Elston Mayhew & Luke Mayhew
Susannah Fancelli
Sadie Feast & Sean Holmes
Jane & David Fletcher
Julian Granville & Louisiana Lush
Lynne Guyton & Nick Dale
Lesley Hill & Russ Shaw
Ann Joseph
Juliet & Michael Humphries
Kate & Kevin McGrath
Catherine McKenna
John McVittie
Zhenya & Preston Mendenhall
Emma & Michael O'Kane
Sherice Pitter
Marianne Rance
Peter Raymond
Janet Robb
Cathy Robertson
Tania Tate

## INDIVIDUALS
Anonymous
Kate Brooke
Cathy Comerford
Chris & Amanda Curry
Janet Ellis
Roger de Freitas
Livia & Colin Firth
Nick & Allison Gaynor
John & Clare Grumbar
Alex Joffe
Sali Lewis
Jon Morgan

Sheelagh O'Neill
Sandy & Caroline Orr
Caroline Posnansky
Liz Rigden
Jon & NoraLee Sedmak
Mary Strang
Sarah Jane Stubbs
Roger & Kate Wylie

## TRUST & FOUNDATIONS
Andrew Lloyd Webber Foundation
Aziz Foundation
BBC Children in Need
British Council
Charles Hayward Foundation
The Daisy Trust
Discovery Foundation
Esmée Fairbairn Foundation
Fagus Anstruther Memorial Trust
Garfield Weston Foundation
Golsoncott Foundation
Hammersmith United Charities
The Idlewild Trust
The Ironmongers' Company
Jack Petchey Foundation
John Lyon's Charity
McGrath Charitable Trust
People's Postcode Trust
Reuben Foundation
Sam Griffiths Foundation
SHINE Trust
Sir John Cass's Foundation
The Tudor Trust
Wates Foundation
Winton Philanthropies
The Worshipful Company of Grocers

## COMPANIES
Barclays
Bloomberg
HammersmithLondon
Horton & Garton
MAC
Piper Private Equity
UKTV
Hotel Partner – Novotel London West

# The Seagull

## Characters

**Irina**, *an actress*
**Konstantin**, *her son*
**Peter**, *her brother*
**Nina**, *an actress*
**Leo**, *an estate manager*
**Pauline**, *his wife*
**Marcia**, *his daughter*
**Boris**, *a man of letters*
**Hugo**, *a doctor*
**Simeon**, *a teacher*
**Jacob**, *a labourer*

*The play takes place on **Peter**'s estate in the countryside. Two years pass between Act Three and Act Four.*

## Act One

*An area of the park in* **Peter Sorin**'s *estate.*

*A wide avenue of trees lead towards a lake.*

*A temporary stage has been built by the side of the lake.*

*Bushes and shrubs edge the stage.*

*Some chairs.*

*A small table.*

*Just gone sunset.*

**Jacob** *prepares the stage for the evening performance. He coughs and pants as he works. He is constructing the set.*

**Simeon** *and* **Marcia** *enter.*

**Simeon**   Why do you do that?

**Marcia**   Do what?

**Simeon**   Wander round like that?

**Marcia**   Like what?

**Simeon**   You look so angry. All the time.

**Marcia**   I am angry. All the time.

**Simeon**   What on earth have you got to be angry about?

**Marcia**   My life.

**Simeon** (*he thinks*)   See I don't understand that. Your life's not so bad. Your life's good. You're young. You're healthy. Your dad might not be the richest man in the world but he's doing pretty well for himself. You should open your eyes. Look around you. Look at my life. For example. Do you know how much money I make every month?

**Marcia**   I have no idea.

**Simeon**   Not very much. Not very much is how much. Not very much at all. But I don't mope around.

**Marcia**   I wasn't moping around.

**Simeon**   And most of it is taxed.

**Marcia**   There's more to life than just money, you know.

**Simeon**   You think so do you? Well think about this. On my wages I've got to support my mother. I've got to support my two sisters. I've got to support my little brother. How do I do that? I give up food for a day or so every month. I give up sugar. I give up tea. I give up smoking. I give up everything in life that gives me any kind of happiness. And I'll tell you it leaves me not so sure if there's 'more to life than money you know'.

**Marcia** *looks at him. Then away again. She looks at the stage.*

**Marcia**   They'll be starting soon. The show.

**Simeon**   Yes. Nina's performing, isn't she? Konstantin's new play. They're completely in love with each other. And tonight their imaginations will join as one to show the world how extraordinary they can be. We're not quite the same, me and you. I love you and being apart from you makes me miserable. It makes me so miserable, in fact, that I walk four miles every day to come and see you. Four miles here and four miles back. And all I get from you is this big blank face. I don't blame you. I mean, what have I got that I could possibly offer you? And with my family, I'm not exactly a very exciting proposition.

**Marcia**   It's not that. (*She rolls a cigarette.*) It's really sweet that you love me so much. Thing is, I just don't love you at all.

You want a cigarette?

**Simeon**   No, thank you.

*Some time.*

**Marcia**  This weather's nice though. It's such a lovely evening.

All you ever do is talk and talk and talk. About the world. And how skint you are. It's the worst thing you can imagine, isn't it? Being poor. There are so many worse things. I'm telling you. I'd rather be homeless, me, wandering round begging than …

**Simeon**  What?

**Marcia**  It doesn't matter. You wouldn't understand, would you?

**Peter** *and* **Konstantin** *enter.*

**Peter**  I've never really taken to the countryside. Perfectly obvious to everyone now that I simply never will. I'll never get used to it. Last night I went to sleep at ten o'clock. I slept for eleven hours. Woke up at nine. It was as though my brain had got stuck to my skull I'd been asleep for so long. (*He starts laughing.*) And then! This afternoon! Dozed off! I'm in pieces. The whole thing is a bloody nightmare.

**Konstantin**  Yes. You're better off in town. Clearly. Much better. (*He sees* **Simeon** *and* **Marcia**.) We're not ready. We'll call you when we're ready. I told you that. Please.

**Peter**  Marcia. My dear. Would you be so kind as to tell your father to let his blasted dog off the lead in the evenings? He howls endlessly. My sister was awake all night again.

**Marcia**  Tell him yourself. Nothing to do with me. (*To* **Simeon**.) Come on.

**Simeon**  Yes. Okay. (*To* **Konstantin**.) You won't forget us will you?

**Konstantin**  Of course I won't forget you.

**Simeon**  You'll give us plenty of notice before it starts, won't you?

**Simeon** *and* **Marcia** *leave.*

**Peter**   Bloody dog'll be howling all night now. Guaranteed. It's a total farce. I've never been able to live in the countryside in the way that I want to, is the problem. In the past I'd take a month's holiday every year. I'd come here for the rest. The air. The relaxation. Problem was, the second you arrive they badger you. The bloody estate manager and the bloody estate manager's wife. With their infernal worries and their nonsense. I'd be desperate to leave within an hour of arriving. (*He laughs.*) And now I'm retired. There's nowhere else for me. Whatever I am inclined to do and wherever I have a mind to go. I'm stuck here.

**Jacob** *enters.*

**Jacob** (*to* **Konstantin**)   I'm having a break. I'm going swimming.

**Konstantin**   Right. Fine. Good. Just make sure you're ready. We've got ten minutes. (*He looks at his watch.*) It's nearly time.

**Jacob**   Ten minutes. Got it.

*He leaves.*

**Konstantin**   This is a proper theatre. A curtain. A wing. A second wing. An empty space. No set. No scenery. The auditorium open to the lake and the horizon. The play will start at precisely twenty-seven minutes past eight. The exact moment that the moon will rise over the trees.

**Peter**   Marvellous.

**Konstantin**   If Nina's late the whole thing will be ruined. It'll be lost. She should be here by now. Her father never lets her out of his sight. And her stepmother is even worse. Getting her here is like organising a jail break.

*He straightens his uncle's tie.*

Your hair's a state. And your beard.

**Peter** *tries to tidy his beard.*

**Peter**   The bane of my life this beard. Even when I was young I looked like a ragged old drunk. It's true. I'm telling you. Caused terrible problems with women. They never liked me.

*He sits down.*

Why is your mother in such a foul mood?

**Konstantin**   She's just bored. (*He sits with him.*) And she's jealous. She's angry with me. She's angry about tonight. She hates my play and she hates that she's not in my play. She's not read my play but she still hates it. She's jealous of Nina.

**Peter** (*laughing*)   You are funny. Really!

**Konstantin**   It drives her insane that even here, on this little stage, Nina will be the centre of other peoples' attention. She's a complicated woman, my mother. Psychologically she is fascinating. She's talented. No arguing about that. The poetry she can recite! By heart! It makes you catch your breath. And she's kind. She's so loving to the poorly and the sick. But you try complimenting another actor. My God! She's the only one who gets the compliments! Nobody else! She's the only one we can write about! She's the only one we can talk about! We must never forget her St Joan. Never forget her Cleopatra. She's addicted to the adulation. She comes here to the countryside and she can't get her hit. So she gets bored. And she gets angry. And she hates us all.

She's started getting superstitious. She gets frightened if she sees three candles lit in the same room. She gets agitated by the number 13. And the older she gets the meaner she gets. She has hundreds of thousands in a bank in Geneva. Or Jersey. Or Odessa. Or somewhere. I know that for a fact. But you try asking her for a loan? She breaks down. Bursts into tears.

**Peter**   You're imagining it, you know? About your mother not liking your play. You're getting all wound up about it. Calm down. Your mother adores you.

**Konstantin** *picks a nearby flower. He starts picking off the leaves.*

**Konstantin** She loves me. She loves me not. She loves me. She loves me not. She loves me. She loves me not. (*He laughs.*) You see! My own mother doesn't love me! How can she? She wants to live! She wants to love! She wants to wear the most extraordinary clothes. But I'm twenty-five! Her son is twenty-five! I'm a constant reminder to her that she is no longer young. When I'm not here she's thirty years old. When I am she's fifty and she hates me for it. And she is furious with me because I hate the kind of theatre she has made all her life. To her it's everything. To me it's arid and tired and conventional and boring. Unless you take great care of it the theatre can be the most tedious, old-fashioned, prejudiced, elitist form there is. You go to her theatre. The curtain rises on these rooms. These horrible little rooms. And everybody's there. Standing in their lights. In their horrible clothes. So wretchedly elegant. And they imagine, they honestly imagine that they can show us anything about how people live. They think they understand how people live and they try passing on all their deep understanding in these vile banal messages and morals in their vile banal plays. And every play is exactly the same. Every idea is exactly the same. Every performance is exactly the same. Every speech is exactly the same. Every image is exactly the same. They make me want to scream. They make me want to run away screaming.

**Peter** Yes but the theatre! We can't live without the theatre.

**Konstantin** We need something new. We need new ways of thinking. We need new forms. If we don't have them then it would honestly be better to have nothing at all. (*He looks at his watch again.*) I love my mother. I love her very much. But her whole life is meaningless. She spends her time swanning around with that, what does he call himself? That 'man of letters'! Her name is constantly in the papers. I'm just I'm so tired of it. I'm tired of it. Sometimes it's just my ego. I know that. I understand that. Sometimes it makes me so angry that my mother is this famous actress. I just wish, sometimes, that she could just be an ordinary woman. Uncle Peter, can you think of a situation more desperate, more stupid than this: she used to have these, these soirees she called them. She would invite every celebrity she could think of. The actors and the artists and the singers and the writers. And she used to wheel me out. Me. A nobody. To stand amongst them. To soak it all in. They only spoke to me because I was her son. Who the hell am I? What the hell do I matter? I left university in the middle of my third year. 'Due to circumstances beyond our control.' As they put it at the time. I have no talent. I have no money. Not a single penny. When she had these parties I could feel them all, the writers and the artists and everybody, I could feel them judging me. Weighing me up. Trying to figure out precisely how insignificant I really was. I could read their minds. It was so humiliating.

**Peter**   What do you make of him, the 'man of letters'? I can't figure him out. He never says anything.

**Konstantin**   Oh. He's all right. Clever enough. In his way. He's fairly, you know, decent person. And he's so successful. He's got everything. And his work's fine. It's fine. It is. It is. But once you've read Tolstoy. Once you've read Zola. There isn't a great deal of point in reading Boris Trigorin.

**Peter**   Well. Say what you like but I like writers. There was a time, in my life, when I only wanted to achieve two things. I wanted to get married and I wanted to be a writer. I achieved neither.

**Konstantin** *signals for* **Peter** *to stop talking.*

**Konstantin**   Is this her? (*He listens some more.*) I can't live without her, Uncle. Even the sound of her footsteps drives me insane. I'm so happy.

**Nina** *enters.*

*He runs to her. Holds her.*

My angel. My dream has come true.

**Nina**    I'm not late. I told you I wouldn't be and I'm not.

**Konstantin** *kisses her hands.*

**Konstantin** (*punctuated by kisses*)    You. Are. Not. Late.

**Nina**    I've been so nervous all day. I've been terrified. I was worried my father wouldn't let me come. But he went out with my stepmother. They took so long getting ready. By the time they were leaving the sun was setting. The moon was getting ready to rise. In my head I was urging them to hurry up. (*She laughs.*) I'm so happy. (*She squeezes* **Peter**'s *hand.*)

**Peter**    You've got tears in your eyes. That's not good, is it?

**Nina**    It's nothing really. I can't catch my breath. Look at me. I'm a state. We've got to be quick. I have to go in half an hour. I can't be late. I can't, God! I really, I can't. My father has no idea I'm here.

**Konstantin**    Don't panic. Please. We need to start. We need to start now. We need to fetch everybody.

**Peter**    I'll go for them. Right now,

*He heads to go. Humming Beethoven's Fifth Symphony to himself. Enjoying the drama. Then stops. Turns to* **Nina**.

A friend said to me one time. He was a lawyer. A public prosecutor. 'You have a strong voice, Peter Sorin. A very loud singing voice. It's a shame it's so bloody awful.'

*He chuckles and leaves.*

**Nina**    My father would be furious if he knew I was coming here. He says this is a place for bohemians. My stepmother said the same thing. She said 'you can't trust these people'. They're already worried I'm going to run away from home and be an actress. But I can't not come here. I'm drawn here. To this place. To this lake. I'm drawn to this lake like a seagull. And I'm drawn to you. You fill my heart.

*She looks around.*

**Konstantin**   There's nobody here. We're all alone.

**Nina**   I thought I heard somebody.

**Konstantin**   There's nobody.

*He kisses her.*

**Nina**   What tree's that?

**Konstantin**   It's an Elm.

**Nina**   Why is it so dark?

**Konstantin**   It's night-time. Everything's dark. Don't run away after the play. Please. Not tonight. Stay.

**Nina**   I can't.

**Konstantin**   What if I came back with you. I could walk you home. I could stand in your garden and stare up at your window until the morning.

**Nina**   You couldn't. Ruby would bark all night. She isn't used to you.

**Konstantin**   I love you.

**Nina**   Sshhh.

**Konstantin** *hears footsteps.*

**Konstantin**   Who's there? Is that you, Jacob?

**Jacob** (*from the stage*)   Yeah it's me, boss.

**Konstantin**   Get yourself ready, Jacob. It's time. Is the moon coming up?

**Jacob**   It's starting to, boss.

**Konstantin**   Have you get everything ready? The methylated spirits? The sulphuric acid? When the red eyes start to glow, that's when we should smell the sulphur. (*To* **Nina**.) You go. Get yourself ready. Are you nervous?

**Nina**   I really am. Your mother is going to be watching! I'm not afraid of her. But Boris Trigorin is going to be here as well. I'm a bit worried I'm going to make a total fool of myself in front of him. He's such an important writer. How old is he? Is he ancient?

**Konstantin**   No.

**Nina**   I love his stories so much.

**Konstantin**   I've not read them.

**Nina**   I mean, I love your play. I do. It's just. Sometimes acting in your play is extremely hard. Because there are no real characters in it.

**Konstantin**   Real characters? What does that even mean? The point of theatre isn't to show 'real characters'. It's not to stage some simple idea of what life is actually like. And it's not to, to, to suggest some crude solution to what life might be either. The work of theatre is to create a dreamspace.

**Nina**   There's no action in your play either, is there? Just words.

**Konstantin**   It's in our dreams, when we're waking from sleep, that we understand the truth about the world. The theatre should be a place where we can wake from our sleep.

**Nina**   Yes! And I like it in plays and stories when people fall in love.

**Konstantin** *looks at her.*

*Then they both exit to behind the stage.*

*A brief time.*

**Pauline** *and* **Hugo** *enter.*

**Pauline**   The ground's wet. You should get some proper clothes on. Get a coat for goodness sake.

**Hugo**   I'm really hot.

**Pauline**   You never take any care of yourself. That's your problem. You're so stubborn. You're a doctor for crying out loud. You should know about the dangers of getting damp and cold in the night-time. You do it on purpose. To irritate me. You were out on the terrace all night last night.

*He sings a bar of 'Blue Moon' to her.*

You were so absorbed by Irina Arkadina you didn't even notice how cold it was getting. Ha! I'm right, aren't I? You're infatuated.

**Hugo**   I'm fifty-five. A bit old to be infatuated.

**Pauline**   That's rubbish. Fifty-five is a perfectly good age for a man to develop an infatuation. You're in good shape. Not too fat. Still got your hair. Still got your teeth.

**Hugo**   How do you expect me to react to that?

**Pauline**   All men are the same. A beautiful woman. An actress no less. You fall down on the floor with your tongues hanging out.

**Hugo**   Round here, you'll find, we value artists more than we value business-people. I don't see any harm in that. It is precisely as it should be. It has a certain romantic quality to it.

**Paulina**   And the women who drool over you all the time. They have a certain romantic quality to them, too, do they?

**Hugo**   There's nothing wrong with any of the women I have known in my life. They are mainly interested in me for my medical skills. You can hardly blame them. Up until about fifteen years ago I was the only half-respectable gynaecologist in this whole district. And besides, I'm an honest man.

**Paulina**   You are.

**Hugo**   Women respect honesty.

*She reaches for his hand.*

**Paulina**   We do.

*She holds his hand to her lips. Bites his finger.*

You're very special.

**Hugo**   Sshhh. This is them. They're coming.

*Enter* **Irina**, **Boris**, **Leo**, **Simeon** *and* **Marcia**.

**Leo**   Twenty years ago this summer. She recited. I can't remember what it was. A poem I think. A lyric. A verse of some description. She was incredible. Where are those actors? What was the name of that comedian, love? Pavel? Was it? Chadin? Was it? Or was it Paul? I wonder where he is now. He was brilliant. He was the best comedian I've ever – He could do this thing. With his arms. Brilliant.

**Irina**   I think he was a little before my time.

**Leo**   Where is he now?

**Irina**   How am I meant to know?!?

**Leo**   Paul Chadin. Nobody like him round anymore. Things he could do with his arms! Not the same nowadays, All gone downhill now, Irina. Oak trees. That's what they were. Now all we have. Little stumps!

**Hugo**   You may be right, Leo, you may be right. Or at least there might not be quite so many exceptional performers any more. Perhaps none the like of the great Paul Chadin. But on the whole, across the board, I think the calibre of actor is pretty good.

**Leo**   No it's not. No way.

**Hugo**   Better, I would say.

**Leo**   You're wrong, Hugo.

**Hugo**   Than it used to be.

**Leo**   Absolute nonsense.

Ah. Well.

We're entitled to our opinion, aren't we?

**Konstantin** *enters from backstage.*

**Irina**   My darling, are we nearly ready to start?

**Konstantin**   Nearly. Please. Just a few more moments. A bit of patience wouldn't hurt anybody.

**Irina** (*from* Hamlet)   'Oh, Hamlet, speak no more! Thou turns't mine eyes into my very soul; And there I see such black and grained spots as will not leave their tinct.'

**Konstantin** (*from* Hamlet)   'And let me wring your heart, for so I shall, If it be made of penetrable stuff.'

*A horn blows off stage.*

**Konstantin**   Ladies and gentlemen. My friends. We are ready. Please allow me one moment of your attention.

I shall begin.

*He claps his hands twice above his head.*

Oh you shadows, who nightly, come to us across this lake. Take us with you as you creep. Take us into sleep. Let us dream of what will be in two thousand years.

**Peter**   There won't be anything in two thousand years. Not at the rate we're going.

**Konstantin**   Then let me show you the absence of things.

**Irina**   Yes. Lovely. Right. Come on! Take us into sleep. We're all asleep.

*The curtain rises. The view of the lake opens up; the moon on the horizon and its reflection in the water.* **Nina***, alone on stage, all in white.*

**Nina**   The people are gone. And the lions are gone. And the eagles. The partridges and the deer are all gone. The geese, spiders and silent fish in the waters. The starfish and those animals too small to be seen by our eyes. All things. All living things have completed their cycle on this earth. All things have gone. All things have died. For thousands of years this rock, this earth has not had a single creature alive upon it. The moon is made of paper. It lights in vain. No cranes wake to cry in the morning air. No May beetles in the lime groves. It is a cold, cold ground. An empty sky. A frightening place.

*A pause.*

The corpses have dissolved to dust. They have become carbon. They are stone. They are water. They are clouds. All of the souls of all of the dead have turned to one. There is one soul. There is only one soul. It is I. I am all souls. I am Alexander the Great and I am Caesar, I am Shakespeare and I am Napoleon. I am the cockroach and the leech. I am every conscious soul. I am instinct. I am animal. I know all that has been known. Everything. I know it. I see it. Every life. Inside myself.

*The phosphorescent light from the marshes begins to glow.*

**Irina** (*whispering*)   It's very symbolic. It's symbolism.

**Konstantin** (*pleading to her*)   Mother.

**Nina**   I am alone.

There is a moment, one moment every century when I open my mouth to speak. My voice sings its sorry sad song out into the emptiness. And nobody hears.

The fires and the lights don't hear. Every morning they are born from the belly of the marsh. They skitter until day breaks. No thought. No will. No pulse. No life.

Terrified of life, the devil himself changes all atoms like stones in the water. Everything changes. Everything always changing. In the whole of the Universe only one thing remains. The soul.

I am a prisoner. I am smashed into the bottom of the deepest well. I am lost. I am out of time. All I know is this fight with the devil. I will defeat him. I am destined to defeat him. And when I do the body will merge with the soul and it will be beauty. It will be harmony. And the time for the free soul to lead the world will begin.

It will take years. Thousands of years. The moon will turn to dust. The earth will turn to dust. But until that moment there will be just horror. Just horror and horror and horror.

*There is a pause.*

*Two red spots appear above the lake.*

He approaches. My enemy. My devil. I can see his eyes. His terrible, terrible eyes.

**Irina**    I can smell sulphur. Can anybody else smell sulphur. Is that part of the show?

**Konstantin**    Yes.

**Irina**    Oh it's very good. Isn't it?

**Konstantin**    Mummy!

**Nina**    He is bored without humanity. He misses you all.

**Pauline** (*to* **Hugo**)    You've taken your hat off. Put it back on or you'll catch your death.

**Irina**    The doctor has removed his hat in the face of the devil, the father of all matter.

**Konstantin** *loses his temper.*

**Konstantin**    Right. That's it. The show's over. We're finished. Dim the lights. Drop the curtain.

**Irina**    What's the matter with you?

**Konstantin**    I said that's enough. Curtain. I asked for the curtain to be brought down. Curtain!

*The curtain is lowered.*

It's my fault. Sorry. My fault. Terrible mistake. I forgot that the work of writing plays can only be done by a select few. The special few. The elite. How could I have been so arrogant? How could I have been so stupid? I'm just a – just a –

*He glares at his mother. At everybody. He walks off.*

**Irina**   What's got into him?

**Peter**   Irina. He's young. Don't be so mean.

**Irina**   I didn't say anything!

**Peter**   You upset him.

**Irina**   He told me himself it was an experiment, 'Just something he was trying out'. So that's what I treating it as. An experiment.

**Peter**   Even so.

**Irina**   I didn't realise it was a masterpiece. How was I meant to know that? Come on! I didn't realise that the clouds and clouds of sulphuric acid he was pouring all over us wasn't just something he was trying out but it was actually a metaphor! He was teaching us something! He was teaching us how we're meant to write. He was teaching us how we're meant to act. I'm just – Do you know I'm just tired of it. All these endless jabs and comments and barbed sneering jokes about me. They would tire anybody out. They would. In the end. Don't look at me like that I don't care what you're about to say. I'm right. He's a self-centred, stubborn little boy.

**Peter**   He was trying to make you happy.

**Irina**   Was he? Was he really? Well why didn't he just write a bloody play? Instead of making us listen to his pretentious waffling ramble. Look. I like a good ramble as much as the rest of us. A good ramble can be really funny. Just don't pretend it's some kind of new form. It's not the start of a new era. It's not an artistic revolution. There's nothing new about the form in that pretentious prattle. It's just a couple of spoilt brats stamping their fucking feet.

**Boris**   All anybody can ever do is write the plays they want to write as well as they possibly can.

**Irina**   Well that's fine. He can write whatever he wants. He just doesn't need to share it with me.

**Hugo**    Good God, you're angry!

**Irina**    Not God! I'm not God! I'm just a woman who's a bit bloody irritated that my son should spend his life in such a tedious and predictable and self-important way.

I didn't mean to upset him.

**Simeon**    I don't think it's possible to separate the spiritual world from the physical world. All the spiritual world is, is the sum of the individual constituent elements of the physical world. (*To* **Boris**.) You know what somebody should write about? What play I'd like to see? I'd love to see a play about a teacher. How a teacher really lives. It's not easy. I'll tell you that for nothing.

**Irina**    Let's not talk about plays anymore. Or the constituent elements of the physical world. Or any of that. It's such a beautiful evening. Listen. Is that singing?

*She listens.*

It's lovely.

**Pauline**    It's coming from the other side of the lake.

*They listen for some time.*

**Irina** (*to* **Boris**)    Sit here. Next to me. About ten years ago, fifteen maybe, there would be music here all the time. Every evening. On the lake. There were six houses on this side. I remember the sounds of people laughing. The shots being fired. And people falling in love. All the time people falling in love. Do you know who the real heart throb was? The real leading man. I'll show you. (*She nods towards* **Hugo**.) Dr Hugo Dorn himself. He's beautiful now. Of course he is. But then! He would stop your heart.

Oh. I feel bad now. I feel guilty. Why was I so mean to my little boy? I feel awful.

*She calls.*

Konstantin! Tino! Baby!

**Marcia**   I'll go and look for him.

**Irina**   Thank you, darling.

**Marcia** (*she exits calling*)   Konstantin! Where are you?!?
Konstantin!

**Nina** *comes out from behind the stage.*

**Nina**   I think we're probably finished now, aren't we? I'll,
I'll come out. Hello.

*She goes to* **Pauline** *and* **Irina** *and kisses them in greeting.*

**Peter**   Oh well done, my dear. Bravo.

**Irina**   Bravo indeed. I really enjoyed your performance.
We all did. I was taken by it. You're hypnotic. And so
beautiful. And your voice! My dear Nina, with your voice
and your beauty it would be a sin, no not a sin, a crime, to
lock yourself away in the countryside. You have the most
extraordinary talent. Listen to me, it is your duty, to all of us,
to go on stage.

**Nina**   Oh but that is all I want. I don't think it's exactly
likely to happen.

**Irina**   You don't know that. You can never know that.
Please. Darling. Let me introduce you to Boris Trigorin.

**Nina**   Oh. I'm so very pleased to meet you. I am such a
great admirer of your work. I've read, I think, I've read
everything you've ever written. I'm so embarrassed.

**Irina**   Here. Sit down. You mustn't be embarrassed. He
might be a celebrity but he's a very straightforward simple
man with a very straightforward simple heart. Look. You've
made him blush. Oh how sweet!

**Hugo**   Should we raise the, er, the curtain back up again. It
looks rather eerie like that.

**Leo**   Jacob! Raise the curtain will you, mate?

*The curtain is raised.*

**Nina**  It's a strange play, isn't it?

**Boris**  I didn't understand a single word of it. Not a word. But. You know? I enjoyed watching it immensely. You were very truthful. Very sincere. It affected me. And the set was really something.

*Some time.*

Can I ask you something?

**Nina**  Yes.

**Boris**  Are there fish in this lake?

**Nina**  Fish. Yes. There are.

**Boris**  I love fishing. Nothing in the world makes me happier than sitting down on the edge of a river as night falls. With my rods and my bait. Watching the surface of the water. Waiting for a bite.

**Nina**  It can't be as beautiful as writing. Surely nothing can capture the joy of pure creativity.

**Irina**  Oh don't be too nice to him. You'll get him really embarrassed if you're not careful.

**Leo**  I remember one time I went on a trip to the Opera. With our choir from the church. The great Silva was performing. He was trying to hit the Lower C. We were sitting up in the gallery. And the bass from our choir, for the life of me I can't remember his name. He stands up. All of a sudden. Picture this. In front of everybody. And sings out, a whole octave lower – 'Bravo Silva'! How did it go? Like this. He went 'Bravo Silva!' The whole theatre went silent.

*Everybody looks at him for a short time.*

Silent.

*They look away.*

**Hugo** (*as though embarrassed by the silence*)    Ah. Well. Yes. Silence on the lake.

**Nina**  And I really must go. I must. Goodbye.

**Irina**  Why must you? Where are you going so early? We won't let you leave you know.

**Nina**  My father's waiting for me.

**Irina**  Is he really? He's quite the one your father, isn't he? Really.

**Irina** kisses **Nina** *farewell*.

Well. There's nothing you can do. It's such a shame to have to watch you go.

**Nina**  You have no idea how hard it is for me to leave.

**Irina**  Somebody should walk you home.

**Nina**  Oh no! No! No need.

**Peter**  Please. Do stay.

**Nina**  I can't.

**Peter**  One more hour and then we'll see you home safe and sound.

**Nina**  Oh I so want to. I can't.

*She squeezes his hand. And then leaves.*

**Irina**  She's a poor thing. She really is. Everybody says that her mother was a wealthy woman. And her father has given everything she left to his second wife so Nina has nothing, It's awful.

**Hugo**  Yes. Her dear, dear father is an utter shit. I don't like to swear but sometimes it's necessary.

**Peter**  Come on. We should all go. It's getting damp. My legs are killing me.

**Irina**  Look at the state of you. You're stiff as a board. You can barely move. Come on. Hold my arm, you star-crossed old man.

**Peter** That bloody dog. Can you hear it? Leo. Please. I beg you. Can't you let it off its bloody lead?

**Leo** No way. He's guarding the barn. The amount of grain I've got in there. No chance.

*As he heads out. Next to* **Simeon**.

True though. The church choir. One whole octave lower. 'Bravo Silva!' Come on, love.

**Simeon** Can I ask you? What kind of salary does a church chorister normally earn?

*They leave.*

*All apart from* **Hugo**.

**Hugo** Do you know? It might be me. I'm not a very intelligent man. I miss things, you see? And I might also have gone quite mad. But I liked the play. I did. There was something in it. When she was talking about how alone she was. And then when the red eyes appeared. The devil. My hands were shaking. It felt new to me. Like nothing I'd ever seen before. He's coming. I should tell him. I should say something to him at least.

**Konstantin** *enters.*

**Konstantin** Everybody's gone.

**Hugo** I'm here.

**Konstantin** Marcia's been all round the lake looking for me. She's insufferable.

**Hugo** Konstantin. Can I tell you? I enjoyed your play very much. It is rather strange and I didn't get to hear how it ended but it really affected me. It did. You're a talented man. Never stop. Keep going. Really.

*He hugs him.*

You're shaking. What is it? What are you so frightened about? And you've got tears in your eyes. Real tears. I don't know what to say to you. It struck me that what you did was take something abstract, to take an, an, an idea, in fact, and turn it into something more concrete. I think that's what art should do. Art should try to give form to the biggest ideas we can reach for. You'll never make anything great unless you dare to try. Look at you. You're so pale.

**Konstantin**   You don't think I should stop?

**Hugo**   No. Never stop. Just make sure you are trying to reach for something important. Something that matters. Something eternal. My life, Konstantin. I've had a rich and varied life, I don't mind admitting that. I'm a happy man. I am. But if I'd had the opportunity, the chance to experience that joy, that possibility of expression, elevation that an artist must feel as they imagine something and bring it into existence! Where there was nothing they make something! I would have given an awful lot to have had that experience. I would have traded my shabby life for that possibility if I could have done.

**Konstantin**   Where's Nina?

**Hugo**   And one more thing. A work of art should be built around an idea. A strong, concrete clear idea. You must understand why you're making something. Why you're writing. Otherwise, when you set out, you'll lose your way. And your talent will eat into you.

**Konstantin**   Have you seen Nina?

**Hugo**   She's gone home.

**Konstantin**   She can't have done. Has she? Oh God. What am I going to do? I need to see her. I have to. I'm going.

**Marcia** *enters*.

**Hugo** (*to* **Konstantin**)   Konstantin. Calm down.

**Konstantin**   Oh I'll calm down all right. But I'm still going. I need to.

**Marcia**    Go back home, Konstantin. Your mother's waiting for you. She's worried. She feels really guilty.

**Konstantin**    Tell her I've gone out. And please. Can you give me a bit of peace? Leave me alone. Stop following me around. It's like you're hunting me.

**Hugo**    Konstantin, you can't go. That will do no good for anybody.

**Konstantin**    Goodbye, doctor. Thank you. For what you said. And– Thank you.

*He leaves.*

**Hugo**    Young people today.

**Marcia**    People always say that. When they've run out of anything worth saying. 'Young people today.'

*She rolls a cigarette.*

**Hugo**    Filthy habit.

I think they're playing poker in the house. I might go–

**Marcia**    Wait a moment.

**Hugo**    What?

**Marcia**    There's something I want to say. I just want– I can't really talk to my father. To Leo. Because I don't like him. In my heart I belong here. With you. It's like my soul belongs here. Help me. If you don't help me I'll do something stupid. I'll ruin everything. I can't carry on like this. I can't–

**Hugo**    Help you how?

**Marcia**    I'm in so much pain. Nobody understands.

*She goes to him. He holds her. She leans her head on his chest. Breathes.*

I love Konstantin. So much. I do.

**Hugo**    Oh. All of you. You're all so silly. You get yourselves all agitated and wound up, And all this love. It does nobody any good at all.

I blame it on the lake. It bewitches you. There's nothing I can do. Is there? Nothing I can do at all.

*End of Act One.*

## Act Two

*A lawn between a house and a lake.*

*It is midday.*

*It is hot.*

*The sun dazzling off the lake.*

*Only the shade of an old lime tree.*

**Irina, Hugo** and **Marcia** *are sitting on a bench.* **Hugo** *has a book open on his lap.*

**Irina** Come here. Stand up. Stand here. Next to me.

*They stand side by side.*

So you're twenty-three?

**Marcia** Twenty-two.

**Irina** Even better. You're twenty-two. I'm nearly twice as old as you. Hugo, which one of us looks younger?

**Hugo** You do. Of course you do.

**Irina** See? You see! And do you know why that is? Because I work. I am constantly alert. I am constantly on the go. You know what your problem is? You never go anywhere. You're here. All the time. You're sedentary. And another thing. My rule. You want to know what my rule is? Never worry about the future. I never think about getting old. I never think about dying. There's nothing you can do about death. Can't avoid it. No point worrying about it.

**Marcia** Did you never have the feeling that you were born hundreds of years ago?

Never mind. I drag my life behind me. Sometimes I just can't see the point of carrying on. I know I'm being stupid. I know I should just shake this all off. Cheer myself up.

**Irina**   Behaviour matters. Performance matters. Doing the right thing. Dressing the right way. That's another of my rules. I always dress properly. I always make sure my hair is prepared. 'Don't you ever just go out of the house, Irina, just go and sit in your garden and not worry about your clothes and not worry about your hair?' Never. The reason I look as good as I do is because I take care of how I look. It is very, very simple. Some people just can't seem to understand it. Look.

*She stretches her arms. Dances a little.*

I'm like a little bird. A little chaffinch. Fluttering. I could play a fifteen-year-old girl, I think. Don't you think? Even now.

**Hugo**   Of course you could, my dear. Now. Should I read on? We got to the bit about the corn seller and the rats . . .

**Irina**   Yes. Very good. The rats. Wait. Give it to me. I'll read.

*She scans the book for the right place.*

'For people of the world to flatter writers and try to win their company is as dangerous as for a corn merchant to allow rats to breed in his barns. And yet they do. When, for exmple, a woman has chosen a writer whom she wishes to conquer, she lays siege to him by means of compliments, kindnesses and marks of favours . . .' Well, Moniseur Maupassant. The French might do that. We don't. What we do is we fall completely in love first before we try and do anything as clear-headed as conquering them. Just look at me and Trigorin.

**Peter** *enters. He is walking with a stick.* **Nina** *is with him.* **Simeon** *pushes an empty wheelchair behind them.*

**Peter**   So are we happy little one?

**Nina**   We are.

**Peter**   Today at least?

**Nina**    I'm very happy.

**Peter** (*to* **Irina**)    We're happy.

**Nina**    Extremely happy.

**Peter**    We are. Father and the wicked stepmother have gone away for the weekend. We have three days of complete freedom.

**Nina**    I am completely at your service.

*He sits in his wheelechair.*

**Peter**    Isn't she a beautiful thing?

**Irina**    Very.

**Peter**    In this light?

**Irina**    It's a beautiful dress. She's tremendously interesting. She's terribly clever. (*She kisses her.*) But don't praise her too much, Peter. Too many compliments bring bad luck. They do. Where's Boris?

**Nina**    He's at the lake. He's fishing.

**Irina**    Fishing. He never gets bored of fishing. Staggering really, isn't it?

**Nina**    What are you reading?

**Irina**    Maupassant. (*She reads to herself.*) His 'Afloat'. (*She reads some more.*) Oh it's all nonsense. (*She closes the book. Looks at* **Nina**.) Something's bothering me. Can I ask you? What's the matter with my son? Why is he so unhappy all the time? He's so angry. He spends all his time wandering round the lake. I never see him.

**Marcia**    He's just not himself. It's his soul. (*To* **Nina**.) Nina. Please will you do something for me?

**Nina**    Of course.

**Marcia**    Would you recite for us?

**Nina**   What would you like me to recite?

**Marcia**   Something of Konstantin's?

**Nina**   Really?

**Marcia**   Would you?

**Nina**   I mean, I will if you want me to. It's just all a bit dull.

**Marcia**   Do you think so? I like it when he reads it. He gets these wild eyes. He goes pale. He has this beautiful sad voice. And the way he moves! His funny gestures when he's reading!

**Peter** *starts snoring.*

**Hugo**   Night night, sleep tight. Don't let the bedbugs bite.

**Irina**   Petey!

**Peter**   Hm?

**Irina**   Are you asleep?

**Peter**   No! I wasn't. Not at all.

**Irina**   Are you taking your medicine, Petey? You have to take your medicine. It's important.

**Peter**   Well I would. If the bloody doctors round here would give me some medicine.

**Hugo**   My dear Peter. You don't need any medicine. You're getting old, man. At your age you're bound to–

**Peter**   I still want to live! Just because I'm old doesn't mean I don't want to live!

**Hugo**   Have some bloody vitamin tablets then. A bit of cod liver oil. You'll be fine.

**Irina**   I always think he should go somewhere by the sea.

**Hugo**   He could do. Doesn't need to. Makes very little difference either way.

**Irina**   What on earth are you trying to say, Doctor?

**Hugo**   I'm not *trying* to say anything. I'm succeeding in saying exactly what I think.

*There is some time.*

**Simeon**   He should give up smoking.

**Peter**   Rubbish.

**Hugo**   Now that isn't rubbish actually.

**Peter**   Bloody is.

**Hugo**   Wine and cigarettes!

**Peter**   What about them?

**Hugo**   They poison your soul, let alone your body.

**Peter**   What does that even mean?

**Hugo**   When you drink you change. Your personality gets all blurry eyed and confused. You even, this is true, you start talking about yourself in the third person as though you're not even yourself any more. Don't you? Well? Don't you? You see! You do, don't you?

**Peter**   Well. (*He laughs.*) Maybe. Maybe I do. Maybe that's a very astute observation. See that's what you get with a richly lived life. The capacity to observe things astutely. My problem is I never lived. I have worked in the Law Courts for twenty-eight years. But in all that time I have never really lived. I would like to. Very much. You have. You're satisfied with your life. You've had your fill. You don't really care either way nowadays. You can take solace in philosophy and astute observation without trying. I can't. I so want to. I want to live. I want to drink the richest wine and eat the finest food and smoke the best cigars. And that is what I am going to do. And there is nothing anybody can do to stop me.

**Hugo**   And take the best medicine? See? You make passionate speeches about your need for a grand life and then cry for medicine like a silly child.

**Marcia** (*standing*)   Lunchtime, I think.

*She walks out. She limps.*

Bloody legs gone to sleep.

*She leaves.*

**Hugo**   She's gone for a crafty drink. Or two. Before lunch.

**Peter**   Poor thing. She's so unhappy.

**Hugo**   She's not unhappy at all.

**Peter**   You know your problem, Doctor? Because you know everything, you no longer care about anything.

**Hugo**   That, your honour, is utter nonsense.

**Irina**   Oh this is all so boring. The countryside is so boring. This life is so boring. It's unbearably hot. It's so quiet it's practically dead. Nobody does anything. Everybody just sits around talking utter rubbish all day and all night.

I mean, it's nice to see you all. All my friends. I like hearing you all talk. It's just –

Sitting in a hotel room, studying my part and learning my lines. There's nothing better in the whole of the world.

**Nina**   It sounds incredible. It does. It really. I can only imagine what it must be like.

**Peter**   Well you're right about one thing. The city is much better. You can stay in your office. The staff keep all the riff raff away. The phones work. You can get a taxi without any difficulty at all. Everything is wonderful.

**Leo** *enters. With* **Pauline**.

**Leo**   Here they are. Good morning. Good morning. Good morning. (*He kisses the hands of the women.*) I am so happy to see you all up and about and looking so healthy and happy and just, just, just excellent. (*To* **Irina**.) My wife tells me you are planning a little excursion into town, the pair of you. Is that right?

**Irina**  It is. We were. We are.

**Leo**  Well. That's just lovely. And how, precisely were you going to get there? We're moving the rye today. All the staff are busy with that. It's the height of the summer work. So who, exactly, was going to take you? Can I ask? Madame? Do you mind?

**Irina**  How should I know the answer to a question like that?

**Peter**  There are the horses from the carriages.

**Leo**  The horses from the carriages. And where am I going to get the harnesses for them? Where the hell am I going to get the blasted bloody harnesses? It is amazing to me, this. It completely staggers me. Forgive me, Irina. The last thing I would ever want to be is rude to you. You know how much respect I have for you. And your talent. I admire your talent so deeply. I'd do anything for you. I'd give you years of my life. I'd give you anything you asked for. Apart from a horse. I can't give you a horse.

**Irina**  Well how are we going to get into town? This is all very odd.

**Leo**  My dear. With all the respect due to you in the world, you don't really understand farming, do you?

**Irina**  Not this again. 'Farming! Farming! Farming! Farming!' It's all he ever goes on about. The farming. I've had enough. I'm leaving. I'm leaving today. I'm going back to the city. You can find me a horse to take me to the station or I'll go on bloody foot.

**Leo** (*explodes*)  Well, that's fine! That's fine! You do that! And I'll quit. Find yourself another manager for your bloody estate. I can't do this anymore.

*He storms off.*

**Irina**   He's like this every year. Every summer it gets hot and he behaves like that. And talks to me like that. I've had enough. I'm going. I'm not coming back. Ever again.

*She leaves.*

**Peter**   How dare he? How dare anybody speak to my sister like that? The rude, ignorant, pig-headed – I won't stand for this anymore. Bring the horses. Immediately.

**Nina** *whispers to* **Pauline**.

**Nina**   I can't believe he spoke to Irina like that. Does he even know who she is? You have to say an actress who has achieved the things that she has achieved is more important than farming.

**Pauline**   Really?

**Nina**   I can't believe it. I really can't.

**Pauline**   Well I have no idea what I'm meant to do about it.

**Peter** (*to* **Nina**)   We'll go and find her. We'll beg her not to leave. That's a good idea, isn't it? (*He looks to where* **Leo** *went.*) The horrible little man. A little bloody tyrant.

**Nina**   Don't get up. We'll push you.

*She and* **Simeon** *push the chair away.*

Oh this is just awful. Awful.

**Peter**   It really is. It is. There's nothing I can do about him. He won't leave. I am going to speak to him. Right now, this second.

*They leave.*

*Only* **Hugo** *and* **Pauline** *remain.*

**Hugo**   Human beings.

**Pauline**   Yes.

**Hugo**    They're so predictable, is the thing. Your husband should have been sacked years and years and years ago. But you watch. That old lady Peter and his sister will be begging him to forgive them in no time at all.

**Pauline**    He's sent all the horses out to the field already. He's always like this. Every day it's exactly the same. If you knew how upset I get about it. It makes me feel sick. Look. I'm shaking. It's his rudeness I can't stand. Hugo. I need to be with you. Please. I can't take being apart from you anymore. Look at us. We're getting old. We're old now. Surely now, at the end of our lives, we can stop pretending. Stop hiding things all the time. Stop lying.

*Pause.*

**Hugo**    I'm fifty-five. It's too late to change anything now.

**Pauline**    I know. I know you. Don't think I don't know you because I do. I know how many other women you have. You can't live with all of us, can you? Better to live on your own. And keep us waiting for you. I understand that. I'm sorry. I'm so sorry. I shouldn't have said anything, You must be so tired of me.

**Nina** *enters. She is picking flowers.*

**Hugo**    It's not that.

**Pauline**    I just get jealous. You're a doctor, for God's sake, it's not like you can avoid women, is it?

**Nina** *approaches.* **Hugo** *addresses her.*

**Hugo**    How's it looking in there?

**Nina**    Irina's crying. And Peter's having an asthma attack.

**Hugo**    I should go and check on them. Give them some vitamin pills. Some cod liver oil.

**Nina**    Here. For you.

*She hands him the flowers.*

**Hugo**   Merci, ma cherie.

*He leaves to the house.*

**Pauline**   They're so pretty. Look. Can I see? Give them to me.

*Out of sight she tears them to pieces and throws them to the ground.*

*They leave.*

**Nina** *is alone.*

**Nina**   People are just odd.

It's very strange watching a woman like Irina, an actress as fine as her, cry like that. And for nothing. And Boris. An important writer. Really adored. He's written about in all the papers. You can buy his actual photograph in actual shops. His writing has been translated into foreign languages! And all he does, all day long, is fish. He gets so excited about it!

I thought people like them would be more proud. I thought they'd be aloof. Stand above us all. Sneering down on us. I never for one second thought they would even talk to somebody like me. Let alone behave like that.

Yet here they are. Crying. Fishing. Playing cards. Getting angry all day over the silliest little thing. They're exactly like everybody else.

**Konstantin** *enters. He is holding a rifle. And a dead seagull. He looks at her for a short time.*

**Konstantin**   Are you on your own?

**Nina**   Yes.

*He lays the seagull down at her feet.*

What on earth is that?

**Konstantin**   It's a seagull. I shot it. This morning. I feel very ashamed. I am laying it down at your feet.

**Nina**   What is wrong with you?

*She picks it up and looks at it.*

**Konstantin**   I'll shoot myself, too, in the end. Probably sooner than most people think.

**Nina**   Are you all right, Konstantin?

**Konstantin**   Am I alright?

**Nina**   You've really–

**Konstantin**   What?

**Nina**   You've changed.

**Konstantin**   Yes I have.

**Nina**   I don't even know who you are anymore.

**Konstantin**   You changed me.

**Nina**   What? That's– You're so angry all the time.

**Konstantin**   It's because you've grown so cold.

**Nina**   And you never say anything anymore unless it's in some kind of weird metaphor that nobody actually understands.

**Konstantin**   I'm so sorry. That must be mortifying for you. Even being in the same place as me must be horrible.

**Nina**   Like this bird. It's obviously some kind of a symbol, right? But, I'm sorry, Konstantin, I just don't have a clue what it's a symbol for. I'm too stupid. That's my problem.

**Konstantin**   It started on the night of my play.

**Nina**   What did?

**Konstantin**   It was such a pathetic failure. It must have been awful for you. And women, yes? They never forgive a failure do they? I burnt it. The play. Every page. Every copy. If you had the slightest idea how desperate I am. Every day you get colder and colder. It's started to scare me. It's like I've woken up and the lake has dried into the earth. You're wrong, you know. About people not being able to understand me. That's not the problem. The problem is that there's nothing about me for people to understand. Everybody hated my play. Even you. I thought you were my inspiration. But you clearly find me ridiculous. I mean, clearly. I'm insignificant. To you. I mean nothing. Do you know what I am to you? I'm ordinary.

*He stamps his foot.*

I understand! I do! I really – I do understand. It's like there is a nail hammered into the centre of my brain. And that nail, that fucking nail, like my vanity and my pride, is sucking the blood out of me. Sucking it like a snake.

**Boris** *enters. He is reading a notebook.*

Now here. This is a real writer. Here he comes. Shh. Watch him. He's got his little notebook. Doesn't he? That's what real writers do. Like Hamlet. 'Words words words.' He doesn't even know you're here but look at you. The way you look at him. Your eyes light up. Don't worry. I won't get in your way.

*He leaves.*

**Boris** *writes something in his notebook.*

**Boris**   Rolls a cigarette in one hand. Drinks vodka shots before lunch. Wears black all the time. There is a teacher. He is infatuated with her.

**Nina**   Hello, Boris.

**Boris**   Yes. Hello.

It seems there's been something of a change in our circumstances.

**Nina**   Has there?

**Boris**   We're leaving today. We probably won't see each other again. Which is a pity. I don't get to meet many women like you. There aren't many women who are both young and interesting. Eighteen years old? I can't even imagine what it must be like to be eighteen. I must have been eighteen once. Logically. No memory of it at all. And it's because of that that my women characters, the young women characters I write, the eighteen-year-olds, the nineteen-year-olds, even, tend to be very thin and unconvincing. I wish I'd spent one hour with you. Just one hour. Watching you. Trying to figure out what goes on in that brain of yours. How does this fascinating little thing feel?

**Nina**    I wish I'd spent an hour with you, too.

**Boris**    Why?

**Nina**    I'd love to know what it's like to be famous. To be a famous, talented writer. Tell me.

**Boris**    I have no idea.

**Nina**    But you're famous.

**Boris**    Am I?

**Nina**    You know that. You must do.

**Boris**    I think something must have happened here. One of two things. Either you have exaggerated how famous I am. Or being famous is just something you don't actually feel.

**Nina**    You're in the papers all the time. Don't you read about yourself?

**Boris**    Sometimes.

**Nina**    What's that like?

**Boris**    It depends what they say. When they're nice about me I quite enjoy it. When they're horrible about me. Or about my work. I can get depressed for days.

**Nina**    That sounds amazing. I am so envious. People get dealt very different lives, you know? Some people can barely get up in the morning. They've been given lives that are dull and drab and meaningless. And they're exactly the same as each other. And they're all unhappy all the time. But some people. The lucky ones. They are given a life that sparkles. A fascinating, bright, important life. That's the card you've been dealt. You're extraordinary.

**Boris**   Well.

**Nina**   I'm right.

**Boris**   I don't know about that.

**Nina**   You're one in a million.

**Boris**   I stand here looking at you. I watch you in the sunshine talking about happiness. And Fame. And this bright, fascinating life. But all I can hear are the words. Just words. I'm sorry. The life you're describing sounds to me like a blancmange. A blancmange that I will never eat. I'm sorry. I don't mean to be rude. You're very young. You're very sweet.

**Nina**   Your life is amazing to me.

**Boris**   I don't see what's so amazing about it.

Look. I have to go and write. I'm sorry. I wish I had the time to talk to you. I just don't.

*He laughs.*

It's funny. You just got to me. You got to me. I can feel myself getting wound up. I don't mean to. Well. Let me tell you. Do you want to know about my life? My bright, fascinating, sparkling life? Some people, in life, don't they, they have obsessions. Yes? They obsess about things. Like the moon. There are some people who spend their entire lives thinking about the moon. Well, I have an obsession. I have a moon of my own. Night and day, all the time, all I ever think about is writing. I need to write. I need to write. I need to write. I'll finish one thing and the second I finish it I need to start on the next. And then the next. And then the next. And then the next. And then the next. I write all the time. I can't do anything else. What is so bright about that? What is so brilliant or fascinating or sparkling about a life lived like

that? I never stop. It's almost cruel. I can feel it now.
Standing talking to you I'm getting myself wound up. And
no matter how agitated I get all I'm really thinking, every
second, is that I could be writing. I'm wasting time when I
could be writing. Look. Look up there. You see that cloud.
I see that cloud. It looks like a grand piano. And there's part
of me that thinks, I must use that. Put it in a story.
Somewhere in a story a cloud floated past shaped like a
grand piano. There's a smell of lavender. I think. Remember
that, Boris. A sickly smell. A widow's purple. Use that next
time you describe a summer's day. I cast out for words. For
phrases. And I catch them in my net. And I trawl them in
and I guard them. In case they are ever useful. I'm always
working. I would love to stop for a day. I could go to the
theatre. Or go fishing. I would give anything to be able to
find some kind of rest. Some kind of breath. To stop. For one
second. To forget myself. I can't. There's always something.
A new idea. Like a stone. Rattling round my head. And I go
back to my writing table. I start again. It's always like this.
There's no peace. Not even from myself. I feel like I'm
eating into myself. I gather up pollen from the most
beautiful flowers in my life and I make it into honey to give
away to other people. I take those flowers. I trample their
roots. Do you think I'm going mad? I may be. Sometimes it
feels like I'm going insane. People don't treat me like they
treat most people. 'What are you working on at the
moment? What are you working on at the moment? What
are you working on at the moment? ' All. The. Time. And,
you know what I think? You know what I really think? All
the, the, the praise I get? All the adulation. It's all a lie.
Everybody is lying to me. They lie to me like they lie to a
dying man. And one day, I swear this will happen, they'll
come up behind me. Grab me. Take me away. To the
madhouse. When I started. In the golden years. My writing
was agony. It actually hurt. A beginning writer, especially
when everything he writes is a failure, all they can see of
themselves is how insignificant they are. How pointless. It
fries your nerves. You can't stop yourself from skulking

around on the edges of the literary world. The art world. Nobody knows who you are. Nobody acknowledges you. You're too scared to look anybody in the eyes. You're like a penniless gambler. An addict. I never met any of my readers but, in my head, in my imagination, they didn't like me. They didn't trust me. I was scared of them. I was terrified. And when I wrote for the theatre and it was the opening night of my play. And I saw the audience. I'd divide them up. The ones with brown hair hated me. The ones with blonde hair didn't really care in any way. It was awful. My God. It was agony.

**Nina**　But there must be a moment. When you get an idea. When inspiration strikes. That must be magical.

**Boris**　That part I like. When I'm working. When I'm writing. And I like reading the proofs. Before they've been published. But then once the books are out I can't bear it. I can see. I can see all the mistakes and the horrible errors. The whole thing was a mistake. The whole thing. I should never have written a word. I get so unhappy. I know how worthless I really am. Then people read it. And everybody says 'oh it's so charming. You write so beautifully. You're so talented. I mean. You're no, let's face it, you're no Tolstoy'. And Turgenev is much, much better. That will be me. Until I die. 'Charming.' Nothing more. When I die. My friends will come and see my grave. 'Here lies Boris Trigorin. He was a good writer but he wasn't as good as Turgenev.'

**Nina**　I'm sorry. I am. But you're wrong. I've got no sympathy for you. You must be spoiled by success.

**Boris**　What success? My writing never made me happy. I don't even like my work half the time. The worst thing is I go into a kind of daze when I'm writing. Don't even know what I'm doing. I love this lake. I do. And the trees. The sky. I can feel them. I can feel nature. It fills me up. It makes me want to write. But I'm not, what, a landscape painter? I live in the real world. I am a citizen. I love this country. I love the people here. If I am going to be a writer I need to tell their

stories. I need to understand their lives. Their suffering. I
need to imagine their future. I need to write about science.
About justice. About all of this. And that. And this. And that.
And I talk about everything all the time. I talk and talk and
talk. I run around. People always encourage me. They push
me about. They get so passionate. They get furious. They
want to know what I think. They want my thoughts on
everything. I run away from them. Like a fox running from
the pack. And when I do that I can feel all that life I was
talking about, all that science getting further and further
away from me. A train running down the tracks. And I'm left
stranded at the station. Watching it disappear. In the end all
I really feel is that I know how to describe the landscape. I'm
lying about everything else. Lying down to my core.

**Nina**    You work too hard. You should stop. Look around
you. Let yourself understand how important you are. You
might not be happy with yourself but so many people think–
They think you're amazing. Your life. And what you've
done. If I was a writer, if I was in your position, do you know
what I would do? I would give my whole life to the everyday
person on the street, like you. I would do that. But at the
same time I'd know that they were completely dependent on
me. They need me to make them feel alive. They need to
reach up to me and see the things that I see. To reach my
level. And I know that if they could they would pull me
along on a chariot.

**Boris**    A chariot? Who do you think I am, bloody
Agamemnon?

*They smile at each other.*

**Nina**    I'd give up everything to live your life. To know what
you've known. To feel what you've felt. I wouldn't mind if
people hated me. I wouldn't mind poverty. I'd live in an attic
and eat nothing but bread. I could live with disappointment.
With the knowledge of my own flaws. But then, in exchange
for all that. As a trade. I want fame. Real proper fame. A
thunderstorm of fame.

*She holds her head in her hands.*

I'm sorry. I feel a bit dizzy. My head's gone all–

**Irina** *calls from off* 'Boris! Boris!'

**Boris**   They're looking for me. I should go and pack probably. I don't want to go.

*He looks at the lake.*

It's so beautiful. It's so wonderful all this.

**Nina**   Do you see the house across the lake?

**Boris**   Yes.

**Nina**   That was my mother's house before she died. I was born there. I've lived by this lake all my life. I know every bit of it. The little islands. Every inch of the shore.

**Boris**   You're lucky.

*He sees the seagull.*

What is *that*?

**Nina**   It's a dead bird. A seagull. Konstantin killed it.

**Boris**   A beautiful bird, the seagull.

Why don't you speak to Irina? She'd listen to you. Get her to stay.

*He jots something down in his notebook.*

**Nina**   What's that? What are you writing?

**Boris**   Just a note. An idea. An idea for a story: a young girl lives on the side of a lake. She's lived there all her life. Like you. She loves the lake. She loves it like a bird on the water. And she's happy. And she's free like a bird. But then one day. A man comes along and, just because he has nothing better to do, he destroys her.

*There is some time. They look at each other.*

**Irina** *calls.*

**Irina**    Boris! Where are you?

**Boris**    I'm here. (*He looks deeply into* **Nina** *but calls to* **Irina**.) What do you want?

**Irina**    We're not leaving. We're staying.

**Boris** *looks to* **Irina**. *Turns. Leaves.*

**Nina** *comes to the front of the stage.*

**Nina**    Is this a dream? Am I having a dream?

*End of Act Two.*

## Act Three

*The dining room in* **Peter Sorin**'s *house. Doors lead to rooms offstage.*

*A sideboard.*

*A medicine cabinet.*

*A table.*

*Cases and boxes and a trunk, ready for departure.*

**Boris** *is having breakfast.* **Marcia** *stands by him.*

**Marcia**   I don't mind if you use this.

**Boris**   No?

**Marcia**   In your work.

**Boris**   Right.

**Marcia**   Everything I've told you is true.

**Boris**   I believe you.

**Marcia**   Writers value the truth, don't they?

If he'd seriously hurt himself I think it would have killed me. But he didn't. So it didn't. I'm braver than people might think.

I made a decision. I thought you might want to know. I will grab the love in my heart by my fist and tear it out at the roots.

**Boris**   Great. How are you going to do that?

**Marcia**   I'm going to marry Simeon.

**Boris**   Who? The teacher?

**Marcia**   Mm-hm.

**Boris**   Why?!?

**Marcia**   I have lived my whole life loving somebody who never loved me back. Just waiting for the slightest sign. I've had enough of that. I think the best thing about getting married is that all that love will disappear. I won't have any time to worry about it. I'll have a whole load of new worries that will be much more immediately pressing. And anyway. It'll make a change, won't it? Should we have another?

**Boris**   I think I've had enough.

**Marcia**   Oh come on.

*She pours him a drink.*

Don't look so shocked. I'll tell you something. Women drink an awful lot more than you think they do. Mostly people don't notice because they do it in secret. I just don't lie about it. It's true. Vodka. Cognac. Only the best.

*She clinks glasses with him.*

To you! I like you. Do you know what you're not? You're not pretentious is what you're not. You don't pretend. I'm gonna miss that. Shame you're leaving really.

*They drink.*

**Boris**   I'm not the one who wants to go.

**Marcia**   Then just ask her to stay.

**Boris**   There's no point. There's no way she'll stay now. Konstantin is driving her mad. He really is bloody difficult. First he tries to shoot himself and now everybody's telling me he's going to challenge me to a duel. A 'duel'! What is he like? He mopes around. He spends all his time philosophising about new forms of art. He's very insistent on it. I don't understand. Isn't there room for lots of different types of art? Old forms and new forms. Why have they got to, you know, fight with each other?

**Marcia**   He's jealous of you. I shouldn't have said that. It's none of my business.

*Some time.*

**Jacob** *crosses the stage. He is lugging cases.*

**Nina** *enters.*

*She stands at the window, stares out.*

**Marcia**   He's not a very clever chap. My teacher man. But he's a good soul. He's completely broke. He completely adores me. I feel very sorry for him. And I feel very sorry for his poor old mother. Really sorry. Poor woman.

So. Let me say this. Good luck. I hope your life is full of the best things that a life can be full of. Remember me.

*She takes his hand.*

You're a good person. I like that you always seemed genuinely interested in me and my life. Send me your books, won't you? Sign them for me. And don't just write 'For Marcia. All the best. Boris.' Write 'For Marcia. Who has no idea where she came from. And no idea what she's doing on this earth'. Bye.

*She leaves abruptly.*

**Nina** *turns to him.*

*She tosses a coin.*

**Nina** .  Heads or tails?

**Boris**   Heads.

**Nina** *sighs.*

**Nina**   It was tails. I'm trying to decide whether to be an actor or not using games of chance. It's not helping in any way. Maybe I should just ask somebody instead.

**Boris**   Nobody else can make that decision for you.

*She looks at him.*

**Nina**   You're going. We probably won't see each other again. Will you have this? As a present. I had your initials engraved on one side. And on the other side the title of your book. 'Days and Nights.'

*She gives him a silver medallion.*

**Boris**   What a lovely thing to do. (*He kisses it.*) It's a beautiful present.

**Nina**   Think about me. Sometimes. Won't you?

**Boris**   Of course I will. I'll remember you in your summer's dress. By the side of the lake. The sun falling on your hair. A dead bird at your feet.

**Nina**   Yes.

*Some time. She looks at him.*

Look. We don't have much time. Before you go. Spend some time with me. Just a few minutes. Not much at all. Find me. Please.

*She goes out.*

*Just as* **Irina** *enters with* **Peter**. *Dressed and ready to go.*

*Followed by* **Jacob**, *who is sorting out the cases.*

**Irina**   I have no idea what you're going out for. Swanning round town in your state.

*To* **Boris**.

Who was that? Nina?

**Boris**   Yes.

**Irina**   Pardonnez moi. We interrupted you.

*She sits down.*

So. Everything's packed. Everything's ready. I'm exhausted.

**Boris** *reads the inscription on his medal.*

**Boris**   'Days and Nights.' Page 121. Lines 11 and 12.

**Jacob**   Should I pack the fishing stuff?

**Boris**   Definitely. I'll need all that. The books I'm not bothered about. You can do whatever you want with them.

**Jacob**   Righto.

**Boris** (*to himself*)   Page 121. Lines and 12. What on earth . . .?

*To* **Irina**.

Are there any of *my* books here?

**Irina**   I think Peter's got some in his study.

**Peter**   In the corner cupboard.

**Boris**   Page 121 . . .

*He leaves.*

**Irina**   Honestly, Petey. You should stay at home.

**Peter**   I hate this place on the days you leave. It becomes unbearable.

**Irina**   But what are you going to do in town?

**Peter**   Nothing. Nothing at all. There's a public opening of the new wing of the Town Hall. That should be good. One or two other similar delights. I'd just like a couple of hours of madcap insanity to punctuate my stale sad existence. Sometimes my whole life feels like an empty cigarette packet.

I ordered the horses to be brought round at one o'clock. We can leave together. You can drop me off.

*She looks at him.*

**Irina**   Well. After I've gone you'll be here. Don't get bored. Don't catch cold. Look after my Konstantin. Keep an eye on him. Sort him out for me, will you?

*She thinks.*

Look at me. I'm running away. I'll never understand why my boy shot himself. I think he was jealous of Boris. The sooner I take Boris away from here the better.

**Peter**   I'm not sure what you want me to tell you. There are other things, I think. Fairly obvious things when you think about it. He's a bright young man and he lives in this hole in the countryside without a penny to his name or anything to do or any discernible future. He's ashamed of himself because he's so idle. And he's scared. I am very, very fond of him, Irina. And I rather think he's fond of me too. But he feels redundant in this house. He feels unnecessary. Like he's a drain on the place. A sponger. It's a very human thing, pride –

**Irina**   I worry about him all the time. (*She thinks.*) Maybe if he got a job working for the government or something. Something with a real purpose to it.

**Peter**   Or maybe if you gave him some money. So he can buy some clothes. Dress like a normal human being instead of a – Look at him. He's been dragging himself around for the last three years in the same battered old jacket. He hasn't even got a proper coat. (*He laughs.*) It probably wouldn't hurt the boy to get out of the house a bit. He could go and travel. See the world. It wouldn't even cost that much.

**Irina**   Well. I might be able to help him get a new suit or something. But travel? It's out of the question. I can't. I can't even really manage the suit at the moment. No. I just haven't got the money.

**Peter** *laughs at her.*

I haven't.

**Peter** *whistles a tune. Paganini's 24ᵗʰ Caprice.*

**Peter**   I'm sure you haven't. I'm sorry, my love. Don't get cross with me. I believe you. You are a very generous woman with a big kind heart.

**Irina** (*trying not to get upset*)   I'm being as generous as I can afford to be.

**Peter**   I'd help him myself if I could. But I am completely broke. Leo takes all my pension and spends it on grass for the cows and horse feed and the strange equipment he needs to keep his bees. Waste of time. The bees all die. The cows all die and they never let me near the bloody horses.

**Irina**   All right. Look. I do have some money. I do. I admit. But I have to think about my career. I have to pay for my clothes. My outfits. They've practically bankrupted me.

**Peter**   I know. You're so kind. You're so good. I respect you so deeply. I do. Just. Yes.

*He holds his head.*

My head. I need to sit. I'm spinning. I feel awful.

*He catches his weight on a table.*

**Irina**   Petey! (*She tries to help him, hold him up.*) Petey! Help me! Somebody! Help please!

**Konstantin** *comes in. His head bandaged. And* **Simeon**.

He's sick.

**Peter**   It's alright. I'm alright. It's gone. All gone. Everything's fine. All over now.

**Konstantin**   Don't look so worried, Mother. This happens all the time. It's nothing terrible. It's just Uncle. It's the way he is now. You should go and have a lie down, Uncle.

**Peter**   I will. Just a quick nap. I'm still going into town. Don't look at me like that. I'll have a quick lie down and then go. Makes perfect sense when you think about it.

*He goes. Walking with a stick.* **Simeon** *goes to help him.*

**Simeon**   Ah! Yes. You see. Four legs in the morning. Two in the afternoon and three in the evening.

**Peter**  Yes. Very good. And at night on its back. Thank you, Simeon, I can walk by myself.

**Simeon**  Don't be so silly. Now is no time for pride, Peter.

*He leads* **Peter** *out.*

**Irina**  He really scared me.

**Konstantin**  It's this place. The countryside does him no good whatsoever. He gets depressed. You know what you could do? Have a little explosion of generosity. Give him some money. He could live in the city all the time.

**Irina**  I don't have any money. I keep telling people. I'm an actress not a bloody bank.

**Konstantin** *looks at her for a while.*

**Konstantin**  Mummy. Will you change my bandage for me? You do it better than anybody else.

*She looks at him.*

*Then gets medicine from the cabinet and bandages.*

**Irina**  The doctor's late.

**Konstantin**  He said he would be here by ten. It's gone twelve.

**Irina**  Sit down.

*She starts taking the bandage off his head.*

You look funny. You look like you're wearing a turban. Somebody delivering to the kitchen yesterday asked what religion you were.

**Konstantin**  Don't.

**Irina**  It's true. But it's nearly healed. Just a few marks left. Nothing really.

*She kisses the top of his head.*

Now. You. You're not to go round playing bang-bang games with guns after I've gone. You understand me?

**Konstantin** I won't. I promise. It was a moment of insanity. I was in despair. I just couldn't stop myself, I promise you it won't happen again.

*He kisses her hand.*

Your magic hands. I remember, years and years ago, when you were still working in the city theatre. I was just a little boy. There was, I think this is right, a fight broke out in our back courtyard. There was a woman, she did laundry, on our block. They beat her up so badly. Do you remember?

**Irina** I'm not sure.

**Konstantin** It was horrible. She was unconscious. And you looked after her. Every day you went to see her. You took her medicine and you looked after her children. Gave them their bath. You must remember this.

**Irina** I don't.

*She starts wrapping a new bandage.*

**Konstantin** I remember there were two ballet dancers who lived in our block. Is this right? They used to come and drink coffee with you.

**Irina** Now them I do remember.

**Konstantin** They were incredibly religious. I remember even as a child thinking it was odd.

*Some time. She carries on wrapping his bandage.*

Can I tell you something? Over the past couple of days, I have felt as close to you as I did then. When I was little. There were just us two then. And you're the only person I've got now. There's nobody else.

I just don't understand why you let that man treat you like that.

**Irina** You don't know what you're talking about, Konstantin. You don't know him at all. He is the kindest, most noble–

**Konstantin**    So noble in fact that when he is told that I am going to challenge him to a duel he does the bravest thing imaginable and runs away.

The coward.

**Irina**    Calm down. You're being ridiculous. It was my idea to leave not his.

**Konstantin**    He's so noble, in fact, so honourable and misunderstood that while he leaves us two bickering and quarrelling he'll be in the drawing room or the garden laughing his head off at us and broadening Nina's very eager mind. He's desperate to show her his extraordinary imagination.

**Irina**    You love being horrible to me, don't you? Konstantin, I respect him.

**Konstantin**    I don't.

**Irina**    I respect him and I would like you to not talk about him like that when I'm around.

**Konstantin**    I don't respect him in the least. You want me to appreciate his genius. But, Mummy, I'm sorry, I can't lie.

**Irina**    You're jealous of him.

**Konstantin**    His writing makes me feel sick.

**Irina**    It's often the way. People who have no talent but pretend they do, spend their lives being snide about those people with no pretensions but proper real ability.

**Konstantin**    Real ability?

**Irina**    It must be very comforting. Is it?

**Konstantin**    I have more ability than all of you put together.

*He tears the bandage from his head.*

That's the problem with the old guard and the mediocrities and the slaves to convention. You grab your position of power and you hold on to it by annihilating anything original because it makes you realise how scared you all are.

**Irina**   You pretentious little clown –

**Konstantin**   Oh go back to your theatre. Your lovely little theatre. With your pathetic, pointless, mediocre plays.

**Irina**   My work is not mediocre. It's not pointless. It's not pathetic. Leave me alone. You can't even write a miserable little sketch. You're nothing but a suburban parasite.

**Konstantin**   Tight-fisted harridan.

**Irina**   You fucking tramp.

**Konstantin** *stops. He sits. He starts crying.*

You're nothing. You hear me? Nothing.

*She starts pacing.*

Don't cry. There's no need to cry.

*She tries to stop herself from crying.*

Please don't.

*She kisses his head, his cheeks, his face.*

My baby. I'm so sorry. I'm such a terrible mother. I'm so sorry, my love. Please will you accept my apology? I'm such a mess.

**Konstantin**   If you had the slightest idea how much I've lost. Nina doesn't love me. I can't write anymore. Everything I ever had, has gone.

**Irina**   Don't. Never despair. You mustn't despair. Everything will turn out all right in the end. Boris is leaving, Nina will fall back in love with you.

*She dries his tears.*

Come on. Enough of that. We've said sorry to each other. We're friends again now. Aren't we?

**Konstantin**   Yes Mummy.

**Irina**  You should say sorry to Boris as well. You don't need to fight him. Do you?

**Konstantin**  No. Okay. Just. Mummy. Please don't make me see him. It's too much for me. I can't bear it.

**Boris** *enters.* **Konstantin** *looks at his mother. She does nothing.*

Right. I'm going.

*He packs the medicine away back in the cabinet.*

The doctor can sort my bandages out.

**Boris** *is flicking through the pages of his book.*

**Boris**  Page 121. Lines 11 and 12. Here. (*He reads.*) 'If you ever find you have need of my life. Take it.'

**Konstantin** *collects the bandage from the floor. Leaves.*

**Irina** *checks the time.*

**Irina**  They'll be here soon. We should get ready.

**Boris** (*to himself*)  'If you ever find you have need of my life. Take it.'

**Irina**  Are you all packed?

**Boris** (*distracted*)  Yes. Yes. Yes. Yes. (*Lost in thought.*) Why can I feel sadness in her? When she's so pure. It breaks my heart. 'If you ever find you have need of my life. Take it.'

*He turns to* **Irina**.

We should stay. One more day.

*She looks at him. Shakes her head.*

Come on. Please.

**Irina**  Oh Boris. My love, I know why you want to stay. I do. But get a grip. It's like you're drunk on her. You really should sober up before you make a fool of yourself.

**Boris**   Irina. Please. I beg you. You're my friend. My truest friend. My best friend.

*He takes her hand.*

You can make one sacrifice. For me. Can't you? Let me go to her. Just tonight.

**Irina** *shakes his hand off.*

**Irina**   What has she done to you? You're acting like a stupid child.

**Boris**   I can't stop thinking about her. I just need one time. I think it could be, it could be good for both of us.

**Irina**   One sad little night with a country girl?

**Boris**   I'm sleep-talking. I'm here talking to you but in my mind all I can think about is her.

**Irina**   You've no idea how stupid you sound, do you?

**Boris**   It's like I'm possessed. There's only one way to shake myself away from her spell.

**Irina**   No.

**Boris**   Please.

**Irina**   No.

**Boris**   Please, Irina.

**Irina**   No. No. No. I'm a human being, Boris.

**Boris**   You could be so much more.

**Irina**   You can't treat me like this.

**Boris**   You could be extraordinary.

**Irina**   It's like you're torturing me.

**Boris**   She's the only person I have ever known who has done this to me. She's the only person who has shown me what love might be. Love can be so young. And charming.

And poetic. And transformative. She has turned my world into a dream. I've never known anything like it. I have spent my entire life hanging around editors' offices. Scraping around for money. Desperate. Then, as if by magic, she has come into my life and it feels like it's what love is meant to be. It's calling me.

**Irina**    You have lost your fucking mind.

**Boris**    Then leave me.

**Irina**    What is it with you all today? Has everybody got together and agreed the best way to drive me insane?

*She cries.*

*He stares at her. Incredulous.*

**Boris**    She doesn't get it. She doesn't understand at all.

**Irina**    Is it me? It must be me, is it? Am I that old? Am I that bloody ugly that you can look right at me and talk about a stupid little girl like that and not think that it is going to break my heart?

*She goes to him. She holds him. She kisses him.*

You poor, stupid idiot. You have gone mad, haven't you? My darling. The most beautiful man I've ever seen. You are the last chapter in my life.

*She goes down on her knees.*

My love. My joy. My pride. My angel.

*She unbuckles his belt.*

If you leave me. Even for one hour. I won't survive it, I won't. I'll go mad too. My magical man. My master.

*He picks her up.*

**Boris**    Somebody could come in.

**Irina**    Let them. I'm not ashamed by how much I love you.

*She kisses him.*

My treasure. My broken-hearted angel. You want to do these things. These mad, stupid, crazy things. I won't let you.

*She laughs.*

I won't. You're mine. This face is mine. These eyes are mine. This beautiful hair is mine. All of you. You are so wise. And so brilliant And so talented. The most beautiful writer in the world. You are our only hope. You have such heart. And such clarity. And such lightness. And such humour. In one word you can create an entire human life. In one detail you conjure a universe. It is like you bring people alive. With the words that you write. And every word you write brings so much joy. It is a miracle. Do you think I'm exaggerating? Do you think I'm lying? Look at me. Look me in the eye. Do I look like a liar? Go on. Look at me. I am the only one, Boris. I'm the only one telling you the truth. The only one who understands how magnificent you are. My angel. My magical man.

You're coming, aren't you?

**Boris** (*whispers*)   Yes.

**Irina**   You are, aren't you?

**Boris** (*whispers*)   God yes.

**Irina**   You'd never leave me, would you?

**Boris**   No. Never. Never.

Look at me. I'm so weak. I'm so pathetic. I can't believe I could ever be attractive to women! How could I be? I mean, really. Leash me to you. Don't let me take a single step away.

**Irina** (*whispers*)   I've got him. (*She smiles. Relaxes.*) But, you know, if you want to stay then we can stay. Or I'll go and you come when you're ready. Stay a few days if you want. Come next week. No hurry, is there?

**Boris**   No. No. No. We'll go together.

**Irina**  Okay.

**Boris**  Please.

**Irina**  If that's what you want. We'll go together.

**Boris** *takes out his notebook. He starts writing.*

What are you writing?

**Boris**  I heard a phrase. This morning. 'The virgin's forest'. I thought I might use it. One day. You never know.

*He stretches. Smiles at her.*

So. Onwards.

Back to the train stations. And the train food. And the train booze. And the trains.

**Leo** *enters.*

**Leo**  It is my duty to inform you, with great sadness, that the horses are here. It's time, my most honourable lady, to head to the station. The train leaves at five past two. Can I remind you, my dear Irina, if you come across an actor called, what was his name, Suzdaltsev, Sudalter, Southall, something like that. I used to go drinking with him. I think he might have been Russian. I think. Maybe French. I wonder if he's still alive. Probably dead by now. I saw him once in a production of *The Great Train Robbery*. I think it was called. I can't remember for the life of me where I saw it. He was just brilliant. So sad. He did this bit. He had a bit. He had to cry. And he did. He made himself cry. Real tears. It was amazing. Don't panic, my dear. You've still got five minutes. There was another bit. He realised he'd been rumbled. Had this line 'My God! It's a trap!' He goes, listen to this, he goes 'My God! It's a tap!' 'It's a tap!' Classic!

*As he speaks* **Jacob** *is busying himself with the luggage,* **Irina** *gets herself ready for her departure. Others gather to help her.* **Pauline** *comes in.*

**Pauline**  I got you these from the garden. They're plums. They're very sweet. For the journey.

**Irina**  You're very kind, Pauline.

**Pauline**  Goodbye, my dear. I hope everything was as you hoped it would be. If it wasn't then I hope you'll forgive me.

**Irina** *hugs her.*

**Irina**  Everything was perfect. Everything was perfect. Come on. There's no need to cry.

**Pauline**  It's just that time passes so quickly. We're getting so old.

**Irina**  There's nothing we can do about that.

**Peter** *enters. Dressed for the town.*

**Peter**  My dear sister. Come on, it's time. Otherwise, no matter what we do to prevent it, we'll miss the train. I'm going.

*He leaves.* **Simeon** *enters.*

**Simeon**  I'm going to make my own way to the station. And say goodbye properly to you there. I should get going.

*He heads out.*

**Irina**  Oh my friends.

*She turns to* **Jacob**.

I shall see you next summer. As long as we live long enough.

*She gives him some money.*

Here. Something for you to remember me by.

**Jacob**  Thank you, ma'am. Good luck to you. Have a good journey. Boris.

**Pauline**  You could write to us, Boris. Send us a letter.

**Irina**   Where's Konstantin? Tell him I'm leaving. I have to say goodbye to him.

*They all leave.*

*The stage is empty.*

*We hear their departure from off stage.*

**Jacob** *comes. He sees the basket of plums. Eats one. Takes it off.*

*The stage is empty again.*

**Boris** *enters. He scrambles around looking for something. In a panic. Being late.* **Nina** *enters.*

**Boris**   It's you.

**Nina**   I knew I'd see you one more time.

**Boris**   We're going. I can't find my bloody hat.

**Nina**   I made my mind up! I'm going to act. I'm leaving tomorrow. I'm leaving here. I'm leaving my father. I'm leaving everything. I'm starting a new life. I'm going to head to the city. We'll see each other there.

**Boris** *looks around him.*

**Boris**   Head to the market area by the train station. Get a room there. Here.

*He writes her a note.*

Take this. You can contact me here and nobody will know. I've got to hurry.

*He looks at her.*

**Nina**   Just one more . . .

**Boris**   You are so beautiful. I can't believe I'll see you so soon.

*She goes to him. She lays her head on his chest.*

I'll see those astonishing eyes. This smile. Like a miracle. This face. My God. This angel face. My love.

*He kisses her. A long, soft kiss.*

*There are two years between the Third and Fourth Acts.*

## Act Four

*A room in* **Peter Sorin***'s house has been converted into a study for* **Konstantin***. Doors lead away from the room. A glass door leads out onto a terrace.*

*There is a writing table. A Turkish divan. A bookcase. There are books everywhere. On the furniture. On the windowsills. On the floor. It is evening. One lamp burns under a lampshade.*

*It is nearly dark. Outside the wind blows through the trees.* **Simeon** *and* **Marcia** *enter.*

**Marcia**   Konstantin! Konstantin!

*She looks around.*

There's nobody here.

Where is he?

I'm worse than the old bugger. It's all he ever says. 'Where's Tino? Where's Tino?'

**Simeon**   He's scared of being on his own.

*He looks out into the garden.*

This weather is awful. It's been two days now.

**Marcia**   There are waves on the lake. Real waves. They're huge.

**Simeon**   It's dark already.

We should have told them to break up that old theatre. Take it down. It just stands there. Stripped bare. It's ugly. It's like a skeleton. Rattling in the wind. I walked past it last night. It felt like someone was weeping from the stage.

**Marcia** *looks at him like he's mad. Shakes her head.*

*Some time.*

**Simeon**   Let's go home, Marcia.

**Marcia**   I'm going to stay here tonight.

**Simeon**   Marcia. Our baby will be starving.

**Marcia**   No he won't. Your mum will feed him.

**Simeon**   That's the third night he'll be without you.

**Marcia**   When did you get so boring? There was a time when at least you used to pontificate a bit. With all your philosophies. Now all you ever talk about. 'Baby, home, baby, home, baby, home, baby, home.'

**Simeon**   Marcia. Please.

**Marcia**   You can go.

**Simeon**   I can't. Your father won't let me use the horses.

**Marcia**   He will. You just need to ask him.

**Simeon**   If I do, will you come home tomorrow?

*She rolls a cigarette.*

**Marcia**   God. You never give up, do you? Okay. Tomorrow.

**Konstantin** *and* **Pauline** *enter.* **Konstantin** *has brought pillows with him and blankets.*

*They put them on the Turkish divan. Then* **Konstantin** *goes to sit at his table and starts writing.*

What's going on?

**Pauline**   Peter asked us to make up a bed in here. He wants to be nearer Konstantin.

**Marcia**   Let me do it.

**Marcia** *makes up the bed.*

**Pauline**   He's getting like a child, Peter. The older he gets.

**Pauline** *goes to* **Konstantin**'*s desk and reads what he is writing.*

**Simeon**   Well, I'm going.

*Nobody pays him the slightest bit of notice.*

Yes. Goodbye, Marcia. (*He goes to kiss her. She doesn't kiss him back.* Goodbye, Mother. (*He tries to kiss his mother-in-law and fails.*)

**Pauline**    What are you doing?

**Simeon**    Sorry.

**Pauline**    Don't be ridiculous.

**Simeon**    No.

**Pauline**    He's so weird.

**Simeon**    Yes. Goodbye, Konstantin.

**Konstantin** *raises a hand to wave goodbye without saying anything.* **Simeon** *leaves.*

**Pauline** *reads what* **Konstantin** *has been writing.*

**Pauline**    None of us ever thought you'd make it, you know. A real writer? You? But look at you. Making actual money from those magazines.

*She runs her hand through his hair.*

So handsome! Beautiful little Tino. I just wish you'd be a little kinder to my poor Marcia.

**Marcia** *is making up the bed.*

**Marcia**    Give over, Mum.

**Pauline**    She's so lovely.

*Some time. He carries on writing*

All a woman needs, Tino, is just somebody to be sweet to her. Every now and then. Believe me. I know.

**Konstantin** *gets up and walks out without saying a word.* **Marcia** *carries on preparing* **Peter**'s *bed as she talks.*

**Marcia**    Look what you've done. He's livid now.

**Pauline**   I'm sorry.

**Marcia**   What did you do that for?

**Pauline**   I just feel so sorry for you.

**Marcia**   Well what good does you being sorry for me do?

**Pauline**   It breaks my heart. Watching you. I know exactly what's going on, you know? I understand.

**Marcia**   There's nothing going on. There's nothing to understand. It's just a lot of nonsense. Unrequited love? That's just in stories. It's in trashy novels. It's bullshit. People should just get a grip. And wait for the weather to change. The second you feel the slightest taste of love. Spit it out.

They're moving Simeon to another school. On the other side of the country. As soon as we're there I'll forget all this. I'll grab the love in my heart by my fist and tear it out at the roots.

*In the distance the melancholy strains of a piano.*

**Pauline**   Tino's playing the piano again. He must be depressed.

*Without saying anything. Maybe without even noticing,* **Marcia** *starts dancing to the piano.*

**Marcia**   I've just got to get away from him. Round here I see him all the time. It does me no good. If they'd just hurry up and get Simeon's transfer sorted out. I'd have forgotten all about him within a month. It's all bullshit.

*A door opens.*

**Hugo** *and* **Simeon** *enter, pushing* **Peter** *in his wheelchair.*

**Simeon**   There are six of us I have to feed now. And the cost of flour! And rice! And eggs! My God, the cost of eggs!

**Hugo**   You just have to do what you can.

**Simeon**   Yes. Well. It's easy for you to say that. It is. You're rolling in money.

**Hugo**   In money? Do you know, my friend, after thirty years of professional practice, when I gave up every second of my day do you know how much I saved? Two and a half grand. I went abroad for one trip. Spent the lot. I've got nothing left. Not a bean.

**Marcia**   I thought you'd gone.

**Simeon**   I couldn't. Your father wouldn't give me a horse.

**Marcia** (*whispers to herself*)   Jesus. Can't you just fucking leave me alone for five minutes?

*The wheelchair comes to a standstill.*

**Pauline**, **Marcia** *and* **Hugo** *sit by it. A broken* **Simeon** *moves to the side.*

**Hugo**   So many things have changed in here. You've turned a drawing room into a study.

**Marcia**   It's easier for Konstantin to work in here. He can step into the garden and think whenever he needs to.

**Peter**   Where's my sister?

**Hugo**   She's gone to the station to meet Boris. She'll be back soon.

**Peter**   I must be ill. If you've summoned my sister. It must be serious.

*He thinks.*

Still won't give me any bloody medicine, will you though? It's a bloody disgrace.

**Hugo**   And what medicine would you like exactly? Valerian? Hops? Cod liver oil? Quinine?

**Peter**  Oh here we go! With the sarcasm. His endless, endless talking. It is completely insufferable. Is my bed ready?

**Pauline**  Exactly as you like it, Peter.

**Peter**  Thank you.

**Hugo** *hums 'Blue Moon' to himself.*

**Peter**  I have an idea for Tino. For one of his stories. It should be called 'The Man Who Wanted.' When I was a child there was a time when I wanted to grow up to be a writer. I never became one. I wanted a beautiful speaking voice. I speak like a vomiting frog. (*He does an impression of a vomiting frog.*) 'And so it may be and that is the way and so on and so on and so on and so on.' In court, my summing ups bored the life out of everyone. Even I was bored by them. I wanted to get married. I never did. I wanted to live in the city and here I am. Dying in the country. With all of the joy that the country can bring.

**Hugo**  I wanted to become an actual Judge in the Law Courts! And oh look, I was one!

**Peter**  I never wanted that. That just happened.

**Hugo**  You can't complain about a life when you've lived as long as you have. It sounds churlish.

**Peter**  You never give an inch, do you? All I asked of you was to get me a bit more time.

**Hugo**  You're being silly.

**Peter**  I want to live. That's all I'm asking.

**Hugo**  Every life has to end. There's nothing anybody can do about it.

**Peter**  That's easy for you to say. You've had such a remarkable life that you're not bothered about anything now. But you wait. Your time will come. Even you will be terrified of dying.

**Konstantin** *enters. He sits at* **Peter**'s *feet.* **Marcia** *doesn't take her eyes off him, the whole time he is there.*

**Hugo**   Fear of death is primal. It's animalistic. You have to contain it. The only people who should be scared of death are those idiots who believe in eternal life. And worry about their immortal soul. That's not a problem for you, is it? And anyway, even if it was, you'd have nothing to worry about. What sins have you committed? None. As long as you don't count twenty-five years in the Law Courts.

**Peter** (*laughing*)   Twenty-seven.

**Hugo** (*to* **Konstantin**)   We're stopping you from working.

**Konstantin**   You're not. It doesn't matter anyway.

*Some time.*

**Simeon**   Doctor, can I ask you? In your travels. What was the best place you went to? Which was the best city?

**Hugo**   Genoa.

**Konstantin**   Why Genoa?

**Hugo**   I liked the streets there. And the crowds in the streets. In the evening I'd step out of my hotel and the whole street was packed with people. I'd move through the crowds. Wandering around. Here. There. Darting about. Zigzagging around. Following the people. Blending in. Do you know, when you blend into a crowd like that, when you properly disappear, it sometimes feels possible to believe in the idea of a world soul? The kind Nina spoke about here one time. In your play. Do you remember? Where is she now? Nina? I think about her from time to time. I wonder how she's getting on.

**Konstantin**   I expect she's all right.

**Hugo**   I was told she was living the most extraordinary life.

**Konstantin**   It's a long story, Doctor.

**Hugo**    Well, tell me the short version.

*Some time.* **Konstantin** *thinks.*

**Konstantin**    She ran away from home and had an affair with Boris Trigorin. Was that the extraordinary life you heard about?

**Hugo**    It was, I'm afraid.

**Konstantin**    She had a child. The child died. Boris fell out of love with her and went back to his old love. Which always happens. In fact, he never properly left her. His old love. His very old love. Somehow he found a way of keeping both of them on the go. As far as I can figure out, from what I've heard, Nina's life was never the same again. She couldn't quite get it to work.

**Hugo**    What about her acting?

**Konstantin**    That was even worse. She made her debut in some summer repertory season in some coastal town somewhere. Then she went out into the sticks somewhere. I never forgot her. I used to follow her career. And actually, for a time I used to follow her around. She had lead roles. She did. But she acted very badly. She over-acted was the problem. Shouting. Wailing. She threw her arms about like she was insane. She had some good moments. But they were moments, really. She was quite good at dying. She was good at screaming.

**Hugo**    So she's got some talent.

**Konstantin**    It's hard to tell. Probably. I used to watch her but I never wanted her to see me. And the staff in the hotels she stayed in would never let me up to her room. I knew how she felt. I decided never to press the matter.

*Some time.*

There's nothing more to say really. When I came home she started sending me letters. Her letters were, they were full of warmth. She never complained about her life. Never. But I could tell she was unhappy. There wasn't a single line that wasn't sad and anxious and sick and worried. And her mind. Her imagination. She signed herself 'Seagull'. That's how she talked about herself. She kept on repeating it.

Now she's here.

**Hugo** What do you mean she's here?

**Konstantin** She's staying in town. In a room above the pub by the station. She's been there for five days. I'd go and see her. Marcia went. But she won't see anyone. Simeon is convinced he saw her in the fields behind the lake yesterday.

**Simeon** I did see her! She was heading towards town. I spoke to her. I said hello. Asked her why she didn't come and visit us. She said she would.

**Konstantin** She won't.

*Some time.*

Her father and her stepmother won't speak to her. They won't even let her near the estate. It's so easy to make sense out of people in stories, Doctor. And so difficult to make sense out of them in real life.

**Peter** She was lovely.

**Hugo** Sorry, Peter? What was that?

**Peter** I said she was lovely. I was rather taken by her. The Honourable Judge was in love with her for a while.

**Hugo** You little Casanova.

**Leo***'s laugh can be heard from off stage.*

**Pauline** It sounds like they're here.

**Konstantin** Yes. I can hear Mummy.

**Irina** *and* **Boris** *enter. And then* **Leo**.

**Leo** Oh we're all getting old. We are. Battered by the elements and the passing of time. But you, my dear, dear lady, you're still young! Look at you! Your blouse is so light! So lovely! You're graceful is what you are! Graceful is exactly the word.

**Irina**   You're trying to sweet talk me again, aren't you? You terrible old bore.

**Boris**   Hello Peter. What's all this? Are you still ill? That's not good, is it? Marcia!

**Marcia**   You remembered me.

*He takes her hand. Spots her ring.*

**Boris**   You're married.

**Marcia**   I got married a long time ago.

**Boris**   Are you happy? I hope so. Leo. Simeon. Konstantin. Irina tells me that you have forgotten the past and that you're not angry with me anymore.

**Konstantin** *looks at him then offers him his hand.*

**Irina**   Boris bought the little magazine your story was in.

**Konstantin**   That was kind of you. Thank you.

**Boris**   You have so many admirers. It seems like everywhere I go people ask me about you. 'What's he like? How old is he? What colour hair does he have?' Everybody seems to think you must be an old man. Nobody knows your real name. They're quite enjoying the idea of your pen name! It makes you fascinating. You're a man of mystery!

**Konstantin**   Are you going to be here long?

**Boris**   Only until tomorrow. I have to head to the city. I have to finish a story I'm working on. Then I promised I would write something for – There's an anthology. Just a little thing. Same old story. Never stop, ever.

*As they talk **Irina** and **Pauline** set up a card table in the middle of the room. **Leo** lights candles. He arranges chairs. A deck of cards is dealt onto the table.*

This weather's brutal, isn't it? The wind is vicious. Tomorrow morning. If it calms down I'm going to head out to the lake. Do some fishing. I want to go and explore. Do you remember the play that you wrote? I want to see if I could find where the stage was. I've been working on an idea. For a story. I wanted to refresh my memory.

**Marcia**    Dad. Please. Will you give my husband one of the horses? He really has got to go home.

**Leo**    A horse is it? Home is it?!? I see. Look, Marcia. They've just been to the station and back. I can't send them out again. Not today.

**Marcia**    What about the other horses?

*Her father says nothing.*

You're impossible. You really are.

**Simeon**    I'll walk, Marcia. Really. I could.

**Pauline**    In this weather? Are you mad?

*She sits at the card table.*

Come on everybody.

**Simeon**    It's only a few miles away. Four miles at most.

*Nobody tries to dissuade him.*

Right. Goodbye, my love.

*He kisses his wife.*

Goodbye, Mother.

*He kisses* **Pauline**. *She lets him, reluctantly.*

I really don't want to spoil the party or disturb anybody or anything. It's just the baby. The baby. Yes.

*He waves to everyone. Nobody quite knows how to react.*

Goodbye.

*Sheepishly, trying not to draw attention to himself, he leaves.*

**Leo** He'll be fine. Salt of the earth that boy. No airs and graces. Bit of a walk never killed anybody.

**Pauline** *raps at the table.*

**Pauline** Please. Come on. Be time for supper soon.

**Leo**, **Marcia** *and* **Hugo** *all sit.* **Irina** *turns to* **Boris**.

**Irina** When the long autumn nights come in everybody settles down and plays cards. Look. It's the same pack that our mother used to play with us when we were children. Come on. Let's have a game before supper.

*She sits at the table.*

It's a very boring game. But you get into it after a while.

**Konstantin** *flicks through the magazine.*

**Konstantin** He's read his own story but he's not even touched mine.

*He puts the magazine down then heads for the door on the left.*

*He goes past* **Irina**, *who kisses him as he goes.*

**Irina** Are you not playing, Tino?

**Konstantin** I'm sorry. No. I don't feel like it. I'm going out.

**Irina** We'll start the stakes at ten, I think. Can you cover my stake for me, Doctor?

**Hugo** It would be my pleasure.

**Marcia** Has everybody put in ten? Okay. I'll deal.

*She deals.*

Pauline.

**Pauline** Twist.

**Marcia** *deals another card.*

Stick.

**Hugo**    Very good. Very confident. Twist. (**Marcia** *deals him a card.*) And twist again.

**Pauline**    Have you bust?

**Leo**    Pauline, let the man play.

**Irina**    You should have seen the response I got when I went back home. I almost feel dizzy thinking about it.

**Marcia**    You sticking, Hugo?

*The same piano waltz as earlier plays from the room next door.*

**Irina**    The students from the acting school arranged for three baskets of flowers and two bouquets to be sent to the stage. And this. Look.

*She takes off a brooch and places it on the table.*

**Leo**    Isn't that something?

**Pauline**    21!

**Hugo**    Twenty-one exactly?

**Irina**    I looked just radiant. The outfit I'd prepared. You can say what you like about me but I know how to dress.

**Pauline**    It's Konstantin playing. Poor thing. He's feeling depressed.

**Leo**    The things they say about him in the newspapers.

**Pauline**    Twist.

**Irina**    As if anybody reads the kind of newspapers that write about him.

**Boris**    It's just not working for him, is it? The thing is, he still hasn't found his voice. There's something vague about his writing. It lacks precision is what it lacks. It wafts around like a dream. None of his characters seem in any way real.

**Pauline**    Twenty!

**Peter** *snores.*

**Irina**   Petey? Are you getting bored?

*She looks at him.*

He's fallen asleep.

**Hugo**   The Honourable Gentleman has fallen fast asleep.

**Pauline**   Twist. Twenty-one!

**Boris**   If I lived in a place like this. Beside a lake like that. I'm not sure I'd ever go off and write. I'd just go fishing. All day. All night.

**Hugo**   Nineteen. Twist.

**Boris**   To catch a perch is the most beautiful thing I can think of.

**Hugo**   I like him, you know? Konstantin. I think he has something. He has. Definitely something. I like the images he creates. His stories are so colourful. They're vivid. I have to say they affect me. They do. It's just a shame that his work feels like it has no direction. He produces an effect. But nothing much more. And you can't get far in writing just through effect. Irina, doesn't it make you happy that you have a son who is a writer? A real, professional writer.

**Irina**   Would you hate me if I told you I'd never read anything he's ever written? I never have time.

**Marcia**   When we're ready, ladies and gentlemen.

**Konstantin** *enters quietly and goes through to his room.*

**Leo**   We still have something here that belongs to you, Boris.

**Boris**   What's that, then?

**Leo**   Do you remember when Konstantin shot that seagull and you asked me to get it stuffed?

**Boris**   No. I don't think so. (*He thinks.*) No. No memory of that at all.

**Marcia**   Mum?

**Pauline** Twist. And stick.

**Konstantin** *opens the windows out into the garden. He stands and listens.*

**Konstantin** It's so dark. I feel very strange. I don't understand it. I feel uneasy.

**Irina** Shut the door, Tino. You're letting the cold in.

**Konstantin** *shuts the door.*

**Marcia** Hugo?

**Hugo** Stick.

**Boris** Twist. Twenty-one!

**Irina** Oh bravo, my love.

**Leo** Bravo indeed.

**Irina** Some people are just born lucky.

*She stands up.*

Now. Let's go and get our supper. Our celebrated literary hero hasn't eaten all day. We can play more after supper. Leave your work, Tino. We're going to eat.

**Konstantin** I'm not hungry, Mummy.

**Irina** Well. If you're sure. Please yourself. (*She wakes* **Peter.**) Petey. Supper. (*She takes* **Leo** *by the arm.*) Let me tell you about how they reacted when I got back home . . .

**Pauline** *puts the candles out on the table. The she and* **Hugo** *push the wheelchair out of the room. Only* **Konstantin** *is left.*

*He sits at his desk.*

*He reads over what he has written.*

**Konstantin** 'The poster on the fence announced the . . .' I used to talk all the time about new forms and look at that. It's all so routine. 'A pale face, framed in dark hair.' There's nothing. No talent. Nothing.

*He crosses out what he has written.*

I could start there. When the rain wakes him up and just cut everything else. Cut it out. Cut it out. Cut it out. No. No. No. No. No. Too long. Too pretty. Too fucking pretentious. 'Oh Boris Trigorin you're so wise and rich.' Easy for him. He's got it all figured out. 'The glass from the broken bottle sparkles on the Weir and the shadows from the Mill blacken.' I mean. That is good. That is good. That is a moonlit night in the neck of a broken bottle. The bastard. I'd probably write something like 'Oh the tremulous light and the soft twinkle of the stars and the distant sounds of piano dying away in the perfumed air.' It's awful.

*He reads some more. Works some more.*

Maybe it's not about old and new forms, Konstantin? What are you talking about, Konstantin? Well maybe, Konstantin, you shouldn't waste so much of your time thinking about form at all and instead just write something from your fucking heart. For once in your sorry, shitty life.

*There is a tap on the window. He looks up.*

What?

*He looks out of the window.*

There's nothing there.

*He opens the French windows.*

Hello? Who's there? I saw you. I saw you running away!

*He goes out. The room is empty.*

*It remains empty for half a minute.*

*He comes back with* **Nina**.

Nina. Oh Nina. Oh Nina.

*She leans her head on his chest. Sobbing, trying to control her breathing.*

My Nina. It's you. It's you. It's you. I knew you'd come. I could sense it. My heart has been aching.

*He takes off her wet clothes.*

My angel. My sweetheart. She's come back for me. Don't cry. Come on. We mustn't cry.

**Nina**    I can hear someone coming.

**Konstantin**    There's nobody there.

**Nina**    Lock the doors. Someone will come in.

**Konstantin**    Nobody is going to come in.

**Nina**    Your mother's here. Irina's here. I know she is. Lock the doors.

**Konstantin** *goes to try to lock the doors.*

**Konstantin**    I can't. There's no lock. I'll put a chair against it.

*He does.*

Don't be scared. Nobody's coming.

**Nina**    Let me look at you.

*She looks into his face. Then around the room.*

It's warm in here. It's nice. Didn't this used to be the sitting room? I remember the sitting room was here. Have I changed an awful lot?

**Konstantin**    You have. You have got thinner. Your eyes have got bigger. It's so strange being here with you. Why wouldn't you let me see you?

**Nina**    I thought you hated me.

**Konstantin**    I followed you everywhere. Why haven't you come here until now?

**Nina**    I was so scared.

**Konstantin** I've been to your place every day. I stand
outside your window. Like a beggar.

**Nina** I had dreams about you. Every night I dreamed you
were in my room looking at me and that you didn't
recognise me. God if only you knew! From the second I
arrived I've been coming to the lake. I walked from town.
I've been outside your house so many times. I couldn't come
in. I didn't dare. Can we sit down?

*They sit down.*

We can sit down. And we can talk and talk. It's so lovely in
here. It's so warm. Can you hear the wind? I read
somewhere, I think, I think I read it 'It is a good thing for
the man who on nights like this sits under his own roof.' I'm
a seagull. No. That's not right. What was I saying? Yes. 'And
may God help all homeless wanderers.' Don't worry, don't
worry, don't worry, don't.

*She starts crying.*

**Konstantin** Oh Nina. Don't cry.

**Nina** It's good. It feels better to have a cry. I haven't cried
for two years. Not until yesterday evening. Quite late
yesterday evening I came to look at the garden. I came to
see if our theatre is still here. And it is! It's been here all this
time. I couldn't help myself. I started crying for the first time
in two years. It felt good. It helped me sort things out.
Everything suddenly made a lot of sense to me in my heart.
Look. I've stopped now. Not crying anymore.

*She holds his hand.*

And you. Look at you. You're a writer now. And I'm an
actress. We've both grown up and gone out into the mad,
wild world. I used to be so happy. I was like a child. I'd wake
up in the morning and start singing. I loved you so much. I
dreamed about being famous all the time. And now?
Tomorrow, first thing, I have to get the first train to a town
that I'm not going to name because it makes me feel very

ashamed. It's the most horrible place you can imagine. And when I'm there all the salesmen and the factory workers and the cultured souls of that town will turn their heads and gawp. At little old me. God life is nasty sometimes.

**Konstantin**    What are you talking about?

**Nina**    I'm playing the season in their theatre. The whole winter. I really should get going.

**Konstantin**    I hated you. I swear I hated you so much. I'd spend whole nights cursing your name. I tore up your letters. I tore up your photographs. And all the time I knew I was lying to myself. We're bound together. Me and you. In our, in our, our souls. I can't stop loving you. I never could. I'm not strong enough. When you left, when my work started to be published, my whole life became unbearable to me. It's as though my energy was ripped out of me. I felt like I had been traipsing round the earth for a hundred years. I'm so unhappy. I wander round. And sometimes when nobody can see me I call out your name. I go to places where I know you've walked and I kiss the ground. Everywhere I go I see your face. I see your smile. The way you smiled at me. When I was happy.

**Nina**    Why's he talking like this?

**Konstantin**    I have nothing. I have nobody. I am completely on my own. It makes me feel cold. In my bones. Like I'm in some kind of cell. Everything I write is empty and dead and rotten. Stay. Nina. Please. Stay with me. Stay here. Or let me go with you. Please. Please. Please.

**Nina** *gets her coat and her things and quickly gets ready to leave.*

Nina, no. What are you doing? No. Please God. Nina.

*She looks at him.*

**Nina**    They'll be waiting for me outside. Don't say goodbye to me. Don't come out and see me off. I'm much better on my own. (*She tries to stop herself from crying.*) Please, can I have a glass of water, please?

*He fetches her a glass of water.*

**Konstantin**   Where are you going?

**Nina**   I'm going back to town.

*Some time.*

Why is Irina here? She is here, isn't she?

**Konstantin**   Yes. Uncle got very ill. We contacted her and asked her to come.

**Nina**   Why did you say that you kissed the ground that I've walked on? That was a stupid thing to say! I don't deserve that. I deserve to be put down. Really. That's what I deserve. I am so tired. I am completely exhausted. If I could just sleep. Just sleep.

I'm a seagull.

No. That's not it. I am an actress. That's what I am!

*She hears* **Irina** *and* **Boris** *laughing in the room next door. She runs to the door she hears the laughter from. She peers through the keyhole.*

He's here too!

*She backs away from the door. Goes to* **Konstantin**.

Don't worry. Don't worry. It doesn't matter.

It's true.

He didn't believe in the theatre. That was his problem. He used to laugh at me and my ambitions. And my dreams. All the time. And bit by bit, after a while, I stopped believing in myself too. I lost my faith. And then the worries start and the problems start with being in love and the jealousy starts and the fear, the fear, the constant fear for my baby. I got too small. I couldn't act anymore. I didn't know where to put my hands. I couldn't remember where to stand on stage. I couldn't control my voice. You have no idea what it's like when you know you're acting very badly. I am . . . a seagull.

No. That's wrong. That's not it. Do you remember? You shot
that bird? A man came along one day. He saw it. And
because he had nothing else to do. He killed it. It's a subject
for a short story. That's not it. That's not right. What was I
saying? I was talking about the theatre. It's not like that
nowadays, of course. I'm a real actress nowadays. I love it so
much. It makes me so happy. There are moments when I am
on stage and I know, in my soul, that I am beautiful. And
this week, since I've been back here. I walk all day. I walk
and I walk and I walk and I think and I can feel, every day I
can feel how my soul is growing. I know now. I understand
it, Konstantin, in our work – whatever we do, whether we act
or whether we write – that doesn't matter. What matters is
not the fame or the success. It's none of the things that I
dreamed about. It's carrying on. Having faith. Carrying the
burden. I have faith now. I have my faith back.

**Konstantin**    That's good.

**Nina**    It doesn't hurt anymore.

**Konstantin**    I'm glad for you.

**Nina**    Not like it did.

**Konstantin**    You know where you're going. You know what
you want.

**Nina**    When I think that I am doing what I am meant to be
doing then I'm not scared anymore.

**Konstantin**    I don't have that. I'm still caught up in my own
private chaotic mess of dreams and of images and not
knowing what the images are or what they mean or who
they're for. I don't have any faith. I have no idea what I'm
meant to be doing.

**Nina** (*listening*)    Sshhh. I have to go. I'm going. I have to.
When I make it. When I become a great success. Come and
watch me, won't you? Do you promise? Now.

*She hugs him quickly.*

It's late. I can hardly stand up. I'm so tired. I'm so hungry.

**Konstantin**   Stay. I'll make you some food.

**Nina**   No. No. No. Don't come out with me. I'll go on my own. People are waiting for me. So. She brought him with her, did she? So what? It doesn't matter. When you see Boris don't say a word. I love him. I love him even more than I used to. An idea for a short story! I love him completely. It burns inside me. It destroys me. Do you remember what it was like before, Konstantin? It was good, wasn't it? Our lives were so bright and they were warm and full of joy, I think. Don't you? And we felt everything so deeply. And so delicately. Our feelings were like the petals from flowers. Do you remember? 'The people are gone. And the lions are gone. And the eagles. The partridges and the deer are all gone. The geese, spiders and silent fish in the waters. The starfish and those animals too small to be seen by our eyes. All things. All living things have completed their cycle on this earth. All things have gone. All things have died. For thousands of years this rock, this earth, has not had a single creature alive upon it. The moon is made of paper. It lights in vain. No cranes wake to cry in the morning air. No May beetles in the lime groves.'

*She hugs him. She kisses his cheek. She runs out into the garden.*

*Some time.*

**Konstantin**   It would be awful if somebody bumped into her in the garden and then told Mummy. It would upset Mummy so much.

*He goes to his desk.*

*He picks up his writing.*

*He tears it all apart.*

*It takes two minutes.*

*We watch him.*

*He throws all the torn paper under his table.*

*He opens the door on the right.*

*He leaves.*

*After some time time* **Hugo** *tries to get in through the blocked door.*

**Hugo**    Bloody thing won't open.

*He pushes it.*

It's been turned into an obstacle course of some description.

**Irina** *enters with* **Pauline** *and* **Jacob** *with some bottles of wine and beer and* **Marcia**. *Then* **Leo** *and* **Boris**.

**Irina**    Put the red wine on the table with Boris' beer. We can play and drink at the same time. Come on everybody. Sit down. Sit down. Sit down.

**Pauline** (*to* **Jacob**)    And you can bring the tea in now too. Right now.

*She lights candles.*

*Sits at the card table.*

**Leo** *takes* **Boris** *to a cupboard.*

**Leo**    Here's that thing that I was telling you about. You asked me to make it. You did. You commissioned me!

*He takes the stuffed seagull from out of the cupboard.* **Boris** *examines it.*

**Boris**    Honestly. I don't remember. (*He thinks about it.*) No. Not a clue. No idea at all.

*There is a gunshot offstage.*

*Everybody stops.*

*Everybody is scared.*

**Irina** *stands. Unsettles the card table.*

**Hugo**   It's nothing. It'll be something burst in my medicine box. Don't look so startled.

*He goes out by the same exit as* **Konstantin** *left. They tidy the table and start playing again. He returns after half a minute.*

Yes. A bottle of ether. Completely exploded. All over my medicine bag.

*He sings 'Blue Moon' to himself.*

**Irina** *sits at the table.*

**Irina**   God. It scared me to death. It reminded me of–

*She covers her face with her hands.*

It made me feel dizzy. Just for a moment. Just–

**Hugo** *picks up the magazine that has both* **Konstantin** *and* **Boris'** *stories in it. He turns to* **Boris**.

**Hugo**   There was something I wanted to show you. I read this a couple of months ago. A study in white horses. Their pigment. How pale they are. I wanted to ask you about it.

*He puts an arm around* **Boris** *and leads him right to the front of the stage. Looking out over the auditorium.*

Because I am fascinated by this. Really.

*He lowers his voice.*

Get Irina away from here. Take her anywhere. Do it now. Konstantin shot himself.

*Curtain.*

**Bloomsbury Methuen Drama Modern Plays**
*include work by*

Bola Agbaje
Edward Albee
Davey Anderson
Jean Anouilh
John Arden
Peter Barnes
Sebastian Barry
Alistair Beaton
Brendan Behan
Edward Bond
William Boyd
Bertolt Brecht
Howard Brenton
Amelia Bullmore
Anthony Burgess
Leo Butler
Jim Cartwright
Lolita Chakrabarti
Caryl Churchill
Lucinda Coxon
Curious Directive
Nick Darke
Shelagh Delaney
Ishy Din
Claire Dowie
David Edgar
David Eldridge
Dario Fo
Michael Frayn
John Godber
Paul Godfrey
James Graham
David Greig
John Guare
Mark Haddon
Peter Handke
David Harrower
Jonathan Harvey
Iain Heggie

Robert Holman
Caroline Horton
Terry Johnson
Sarah Kane
Barrie Keeffe
Doug Lucie
Anders Lustgarten
David Mamet
Patrick Marber
Martin McDonagh
Arthur Miller
D. C. Moore
Tom Murphy
Phyllis Nagy
Anthony Neilson
Peter Nichols
Joe Orton
Joe Penhall
Luigi Pirandello
Stephen Poliakoff
Lucy Prebble
Peter Quilter
Mark Ravenhill
Philip Ridley
Willy Russell
Jean-Paul Sartre
Sam Shepard
Martin Sherman
Wole Soyinka
Simon Stephens
Peter Straughan
Kate Tempest
Theatre Workshop
Judy Upton
Timberlake Wertenbaker
Roy Williams
Snoo Wilson
Frances Ya-Chu Cowhig
Benjamin Zephaniah

For a complete listing of Bloomsbury
Methuen Drama titles, visit:

**www.bloomsbury.com/drama**

Follow us on Twitter and keep up to date
with our news and publications
**@MethuenDrama**